The Lion Storyteller Family Bible

For my family. B.H.

Text copyright © 2020 Bob Hartman
Illustrations copyright © 2008, 2009, 2010, 2011, 2015 Krisztina Kállai Nagy
This edition copyright © 2020 Lion Hudson IP Limited

The right of Bob Hartman to be identified as the author of this work and of Krisztina Kállai Nagy to be identified as the illustrator of this work has been asserted by them in accordance with the Copyright, Designs and Patents Act 1988.

All rights reserved. No part of this publication may be reproduced or transmitted in any form or by any means, electronic or mechanical, including photocopy, recording, or any information storage and retrieval system, without permission in writing from the publisher.

Published by
Lion Hudson Limited
Wilkinson House, Jordan Hill Business Park
Banbury Road, Oxford OX2 8DR, England
www.lionhudson.com

ISBN 978 0 7459 7842 0

First edition 2020

A catalogue record for this book is available from the British Library

Printed and bound in China, January 2020, LH54

The Lion Storyteller Family Bible

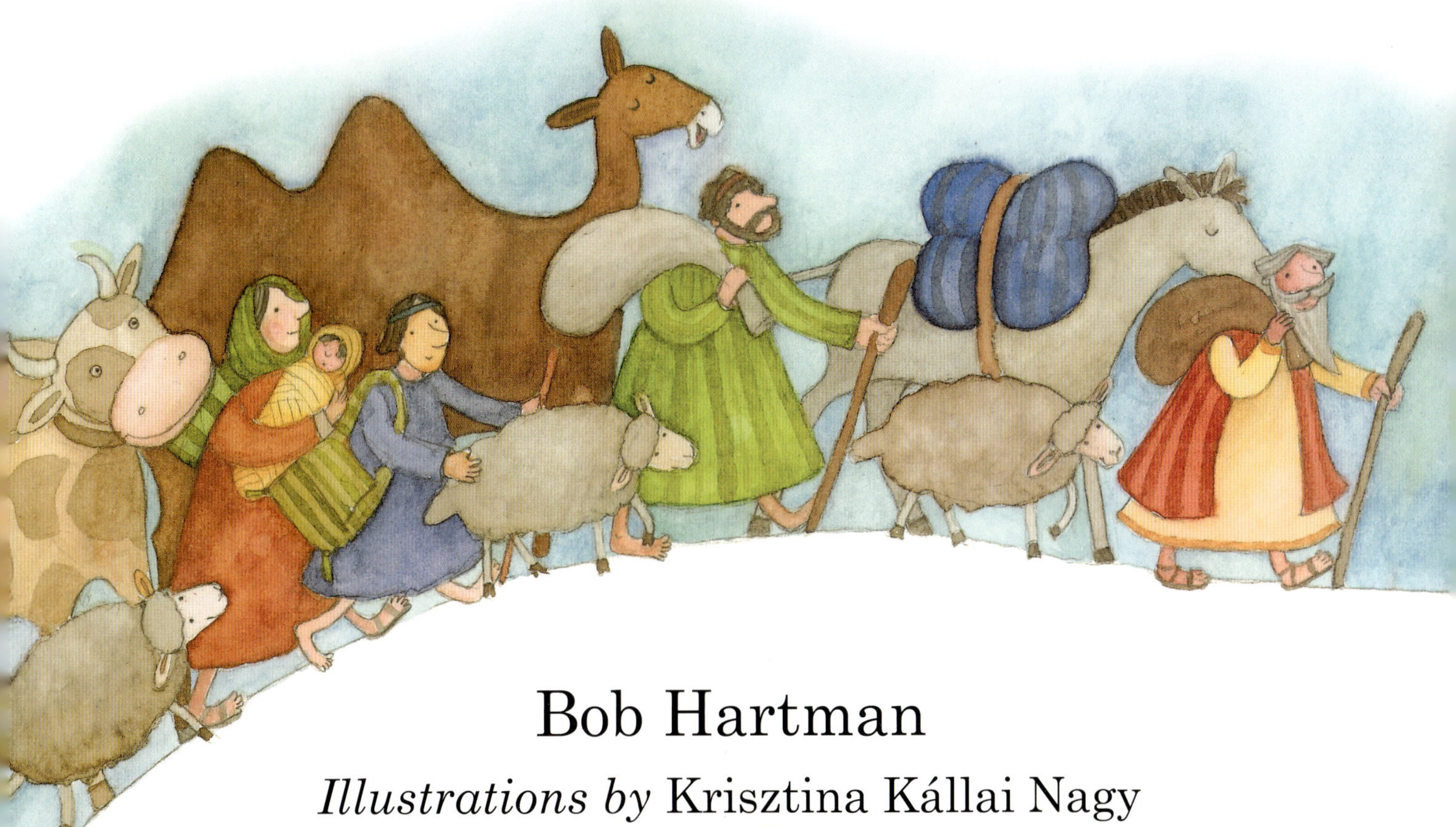

Bob Hartman
Illustrations by Krisztina Kállai Nagy

Contents

How to Use This Book 6

The Old Testament

In the Beginning 8
The story of creation: Genesis 1–2

A Sad Day 12
The story of the fall: Genesis 3

A Special Promise 16
The story of Noah: Genesis 6–9

God's Friend 20
The call of Abraham: Genesis 12, 17–18, 21

The Runaway 24
The story of Jacob and Laban: Genesis 28–29, 33

Joseph the Dreamer 28
The story of Joseph: Genesis 37–45

The Great Escape 34
The story of the exodus: Exodus 3–4, 7–14

The Walls Fall Down 40
The battle of Jericho: Joshua 5–6

A Brave and Mighty Man 44
The story of Gideon: Judges 6–7

Ruth Finds a New Home 48
The story of a foreigner: Ruth 1–4

Samuel Hears a Voice 52
The call of Samuel: 1 Samuel 3

David the Giant-Killer 56
The story of David and Goliath: 1 Samuel 17

The Wise King 60
The wisdom of Solomon: 1 Kings 3

God Sends Fire 64
Elijah and the prophets of Baal: 1 Kings 17–18

Jonah the Groaner 68
The story of Jonah: Jonah

Daniel and the Lions 72
Daniel in the lions' den: Daniel 6

Esther Was a Star 76
A Jewish girl saves her people: Esther 2–9

The New Testament

A Surprise for Mary 80
An angel visits Mary: Luke 1

Time to Be Counted 84
The birth of Jesus: Luke 2

A Flock of Angels 88
The story of the shepherds: Luke 2

The Wise Men's Visit 90
The story of the wise men: Matthew 2

Jesus is Baptized 94
The baptism of Jesus: Matthew 3, Mark 1, Luke 3, John 1

Jesus' Special Friends 98
Jesus calls the first disciples: Luke 5

"I Can See!" 102
Jesus heals a blind man: John 9

"Time to Get Up" 106
The story of Jairus' daughter: Matthew 9, Mark 5, Luke 8

The Marvellous Picnic 110
Jesus feeds five thousand people: Matthew 14, Mark 6, Luke 9, John 6

Jesus and the Children 114
Jesus blesses little children: Matthew 19, Mark 10, Luke 18

Jesus and the Taxman 116
Jesus and Zacchaeus: Luke 19

The Father and His Two Sons . . 120
The parable of the lost son: Luke 15

The Kind Stranger 124
The parable of the good Samaritan: Luke 10

The Wise and Foolish Builders . . 128
The parable of the two builders: Matthew 7, Luke 6

Jesus Rides a Donkey Down the Hill
. . . . 130
The story of Palm Sunday: Matthew 21, Mark 11, Luke 19, John 12

An Important Meal 134
The Last Supper and a betrayal: Matthew 26, Mark 14, Luke 22, John 13

A Dreadful Day 136
The story of Good Friday: Matthew 27, Mark 15, Luke 23, John 19

A Happy Day 140
The story of Easter: Matthew 28, Mark 16, Luke 24, John 20

Walking and Talking – and Shocking!
. . . . 142
A resurrection appearance: Luke 24

Goodbye at Last 146
Jesus appears to his friends: Matthew 28, Mark 16, Luke 24, John 21

The Helper Arrives 148
The story of Pentecost: Acts 2

On the Road to Damascus 152
Paul's conversion: Acts 7–9

The Earth Shakes 155
Paul and Silas in prison: Acts 16

New Heaven, New Earth 158
A Vision of What's to Come: Revelation 21

5

How to Use This Book

 Bible people introduce themselves and their stories, and encourage you to see things from their perspective.

 As you read the stories, you might want to act them out. Be as creative and expressive as you wish.

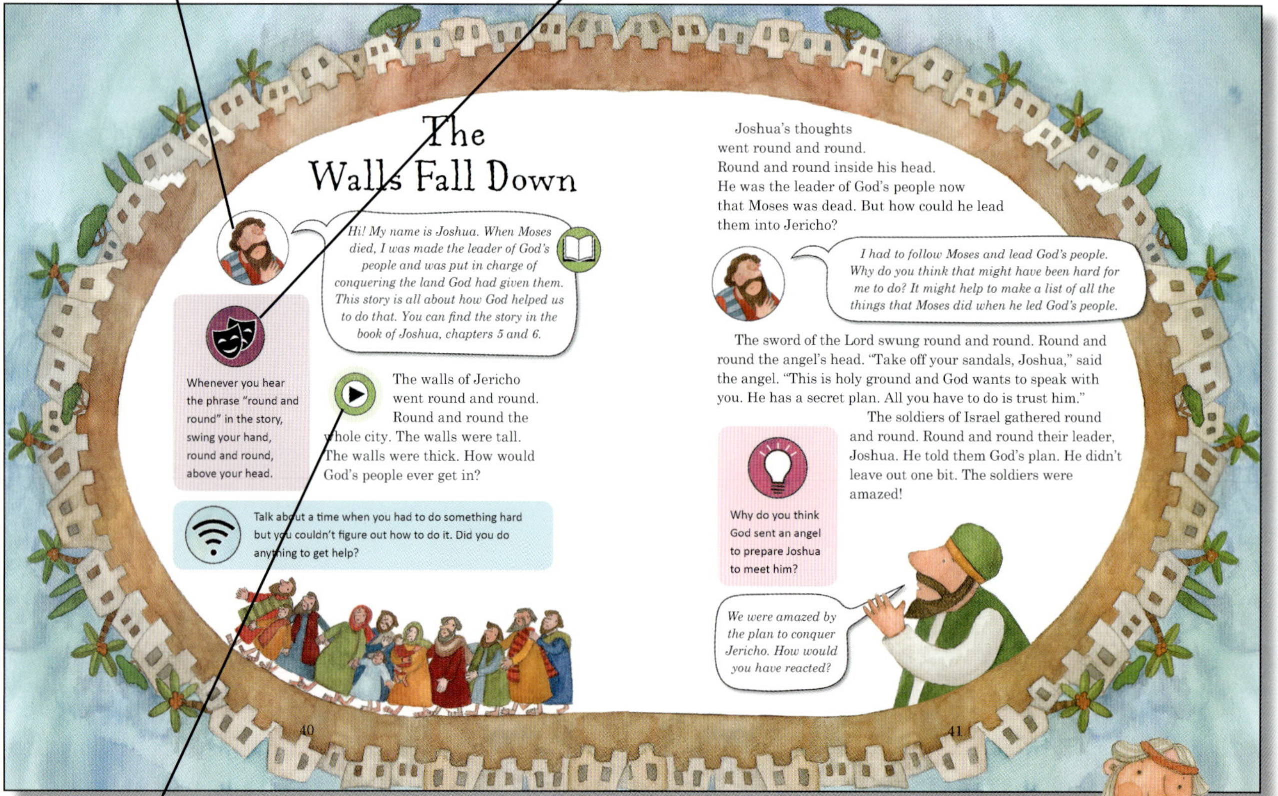

Read the story together. You will find some questions to think about as you read it.

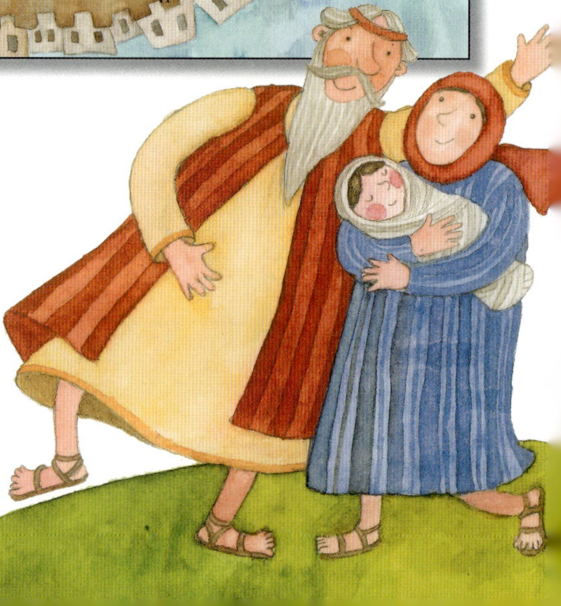

After reading the story, chat together about some of these topics. Parents and carers, please choose the topics that are appropriate for your children's level of understanding.

The Bible is more a book about US and less a book about ME. Have a pad of paper and a pen to write down the relationships (USes) you can find in each of the stories.

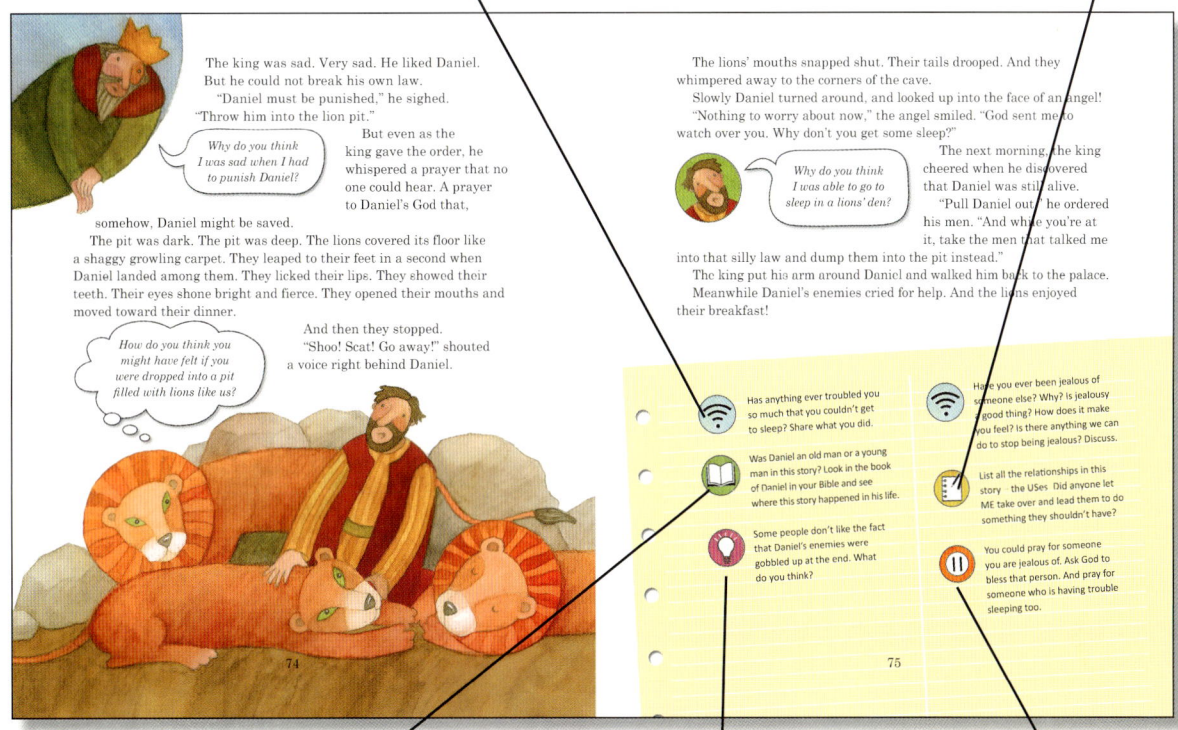

Sometimes it's best to go back to the source. You can read more details about the story in the Bible.

Look out for questions to think about together. Parents and carers, please choose the questions that are appropriate for your children's level of understanding.

When you have finished, you might want to pause for a moment to pray. These are prayer suggestions that are related to the stories.

 *Many of the questions and talking topics can be used by those with or without a Christian faith. However, there are some that go deeper for those who are Christians. Please choose to use these, if you wish.*

In the Beginning

Hi! We're the very first woman and the very first man, and this is the story of how God made everything – us included! If you want to read the story in the Bible, it's in Genesis, chapters 1 to 2.

As you read the story, you might want to act it out. You could pretend to be plants wriggling up out of the ground, and fish and birds and animals. Be whatever you like. Then, when the story is finished, write down which plants and fish and birds and animals you like best.

At first, there wasn't anything at all. Nothing! So God set to work. God the Father. God the Son. And God the Holy Spirit.

But he didn't use his hands or a special machine. He spoke, that's all. He said, "I'd like some light." And there was light. Brighter than a summer morning or a thousand Christmas candles.

God spoke again. He said, "Sky. I'd like some sky. And some water underneath." And, sure enough, there it was. The bright blue sky. With the dark blue heavens above it. And the blue-green sea below.

"Earth." That's what God said next, hard and firm, as if he really meant it. And the blue-green waters parted, and there was dry land underneath. Great patches of it, dirt, black and brown. Here and there, all over the world.

"We need some colour," God whispered, as if he were thinking out loud. And, quivering with excitement, green growing things crept right

Which growing thing do you like best? Why?

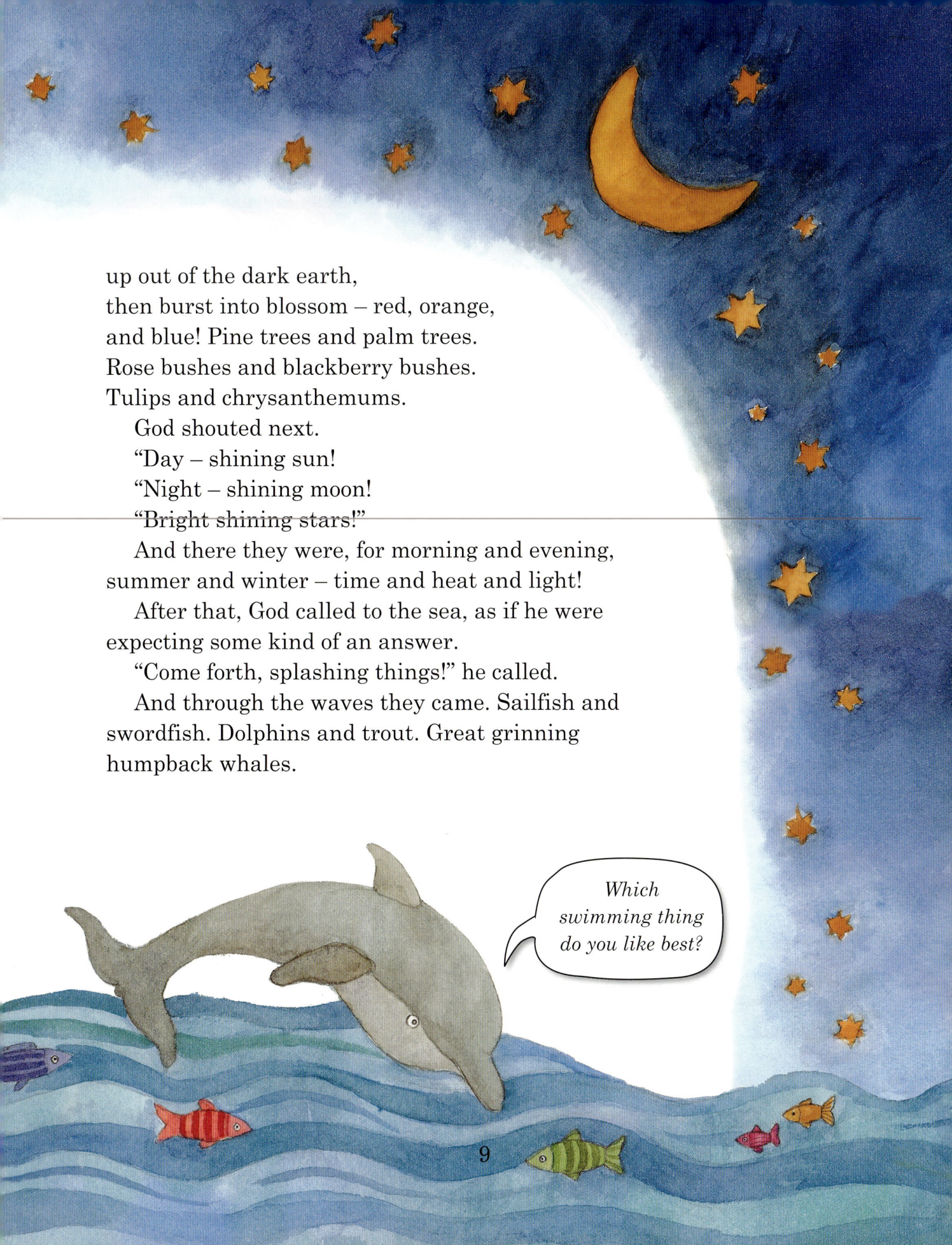

up out of the dark earth,
then burst into blossom – red, orange,
and blue! Pine trees and palm trees.
Rose bushes and blackberry bushes.
Tulips and chrysanthemums.

God shouted next.

"Day – shining sun!

"Night – shining moon!

"Bright shining stars!"

And there they were, for morning and evening, summer and winter – time and heat and light!

After that, God called to the sea, as if he were expecting some kind of an answer.

"Come forth, splashing things!" he called.

And through the waves they came. Sailfish and swordfish. Dolphins and trout. Great grinning humpback whales.

> Which swimming thing do you like best?

Then God called to the sky.
"Come forth, flying things!"
And through the clouds they came.
Flying high and flying low. Flying large and flying small.
Eagles and insects. Hummingbirds and hawks.

Which flying thing do you like best?

Finally, God called to the earth.
"Come forth, walking things, crawling things, running, hopping, climbing things!"
And sure enough, they came. Up from burrows. Down from trees. Out of the tall grass, and across the open plains.

Which animal do you like best?

Now everything was ready. Good and ready. So God spoke again.

"Man and woman," is what he said, as if he were calling the names of his very best friends.

And out of the dust came Adam and Eve. To enjoy all that God had made. To take care of it for him. And to talk with him.

"This is the way things ought to be," God said at last. "This is what I call good!"

 The story says that man and woman were made in the image of God. What do you think that means? What does it say about you and how much you and every other human being are worth?

 Why does God make man and woman at the end of the story? Is there something special about us? What do you think God meant when he asked us to take care of this world? How can we do a better job of that?

 How many relationships (USes) can you find in this story?

 Why not thank God for one of the things you mentioned that you like best? Why not ask him to help you and the rest of us take better care of the world he gave us?

A Sad Day

▶ "Welcome to my world!" God said to Adam. "It's good, isn't it?"
"Welcome to my garden!" God said to Eve. "This is the most beautiful place of all. And I want it to be your home. Take care of the animals for me. Take care of the plants. And eat whatever you like. There are plenty of trees to pick from."

God gave us work to do. What kind of work was it? Is it the kind of work you would like to do? Why do you think God gives us this work?

Adam and Eve didn't know what to say. They looked at the garden. They looked at each other. And then they smiled the world's first smile.

Life was going to be beautiful here. Just beautiful.

The garden God gave us was beautiful. What do you think was beautiful about it? What would a beautiful place look like for you?

"There's just one more thing," God said. "Do you see that tree over there? The one in the middle of the garden?

Well, the fruit on that tree is not good for you. If you eat it, you will make me very unhappy. And you will have to leave this beautiful place."

Adam and Eve looked at each other again. With so many trees to choose from, that hardly seemed to be a problem.

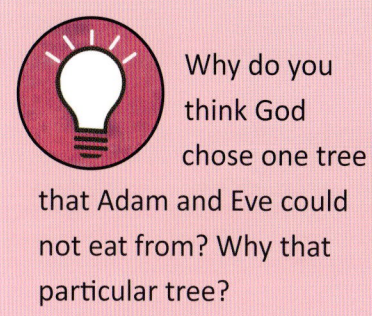

Why do you think God chose one tree that Adam and Eve could not eat from? Why that particular tree?

And for a long time, they were content with soft juicy pears, sweet thick-skinned oranges, and ripe red cherries.

Then, one day, the serpent came to visit. "Tell me," the serpent said to Eve, "which trees are you allowed to eat from?"

"Every tree!" Eve smiled. "Except the one in the middle of the garden."

"Oh?" said the crafty serpent. "And why is that?"

"Because it would make God unhappy," Eve answered. "And we would have to leave this beautiful place."

"Ridiculous!" laughed the serpent. "God does not want you to eat the fruit from that tree because he knows it would make you as clever as he is. You know all about being good. But God has told you nothing about what it means to be bad. Eat the fruit and you will know all about that too!"

A tempter is someone who tries to talk someone else into doing something that is wrong. What trick did the serpent use to get Eve to disobey God? Has anyone ever tried to get you to do something wrong? Was it a voice from another person? Or was it a voice from somewhere inside you?

Eve thought that the fruit looked delicious. She had sometimes wondered what it tasted like. And it wasn't really fair of God to keep things from them, was it?

So she picked a piece, took a bite, and gave Adam a taste as well.

And right away, they discovered what it meant to do something bad. Their stomachs churned with guilt. Their faces turned red with shame. And they realized something they had never noticed before. "We're naked!" they cried. They sewed themselves some simple clothes from fig leaves. Instead of running to meet God when he next visited the garden, they ran away to hide.

Have you ever done anything you were ashamed of? What does that feel like? What does guilt feel like? Why do you think we hid from God? Can you hide from God?

"You have eaten from the tree, haven't you?" God said. "The one in the middle of the garden."
"It was the woman's fault!" cried Adam. "The woman you gave me!"

"It wasn't my fault!" Eve replied. "The serpent tricked me!"

Why do you think Adam blamed me and I blamed the serpent? Has anyone ever blamed you for something? Have you ever blamed someone else?

"You will all be punished," God sighed. "The serpent will crawl on the ground. Eve will have pain when she has children. Adam will have to scratch hard at the earth for food to eat. You will have to leave this beautiful place.

"And when your lives end," God said finally, "you will go back to the ground from which you came."

Adam and Eve looked at each other. Then they walked sadly out of the garden. They had learned what it means to be bad. They had changed God's good world for ever.

Talk about ways that might help us to make the right choice when a voice inside or a voice from the outside tries to get us to do something wrong.

One of the other things that God tells the serpent is that he will hurt the heel of one of Eve's children, but the child will crush the serpent's head. Do you have any idea whom God might have been talking about?

Adam and Eve had to leave the garden. God even put an angel with a sword at the gate, so they could not return and eat from the Tree of Life and live for ever. There doesn't seem to have been a way back for them. What has God done to help us deal with our sins and find our way to a perfect place back with him?

List the USes (the relationships) in this story. How do the relationships get broken? How does ME play a part in that?

You could pray for help when those voices try to get you to do something wrong. Pray for each other too.

15

A Special Promise

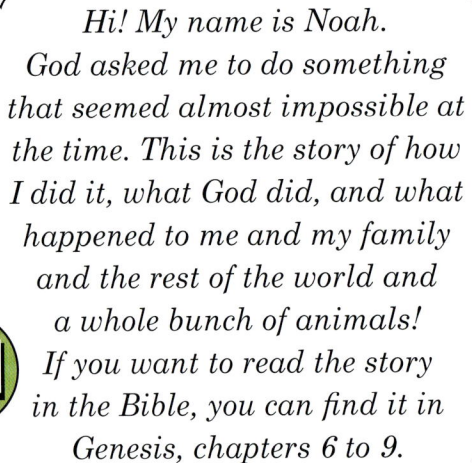

Hi! My name is Noah. God asked me to do something that seemed almost impossible at the time. This is the story of how I did it, what God did, and what happened to me and my family and the rest of the world and a whole bunch of animals! If you want to read the story in the Bible, you can find it in Genesis, chapters 6 to 9.

 As the animals parade into the ark, you might want to choose one and make their sound. Make it when the boat comes to a rest as well, and also when they come out of the ark.

 God was sad. Very sad. Everywhere he looked, he saw people making bad choices. Hating each other. Hurting each other. Making a mess of his beautiful world.

"I need to start all over again," God decided. And that's when he talked to Noah.

Noah was not like the rest. He was a good man and God knew it. So God told him to build a boat. A boat big enough to hold:

Noah,
his wife,
his three sons,
their wives,
    a male and a female of every animal in the world,
        and enough food to feed all of them for a very
            long time!

 *Can you figure out how big my boat was? The measurements are in Genesis, chapter 6. (Hint – a cubit is equal to 18 inches.) Think of something that is roughly the size of the ark.*

Noah's family was surprised when he told them what he was going to do.

Noah's neighbours thought it strange of him to build a boat so far from the sea.

And it wasn't easy chasing, and catching, and cleaning up after all those animals.

But Noah was a good man. He did what God told him – even when it was hard.

At last, when they were all tucked safely away in the boat, God shut the door. Then it started to rain.

It rained for forty days.

It rained for forty nights.

It rained harder than Noah had ever seen it rain before.

It rained so hard that the streams, and the rivers, and even the seas burst their banks and began to flood. Soon every sandy beach, every rocky path, every patch of muddy earth had disappeared beneath the water.

And the boat began to float.

It floated above the houses. It floated above the trees. It floated above the hills, and then above the mountains too.

> Has God ever asked you to do something you thought was hard? What was it? Why was it hard? Did anyone make trouble for you because of it? What did you do? How did you keep going?

What do you think Noah and his family thought about while they were in the ark? What do you imagine they did?

The boat floated for days and weeks and months.

And then it stopped, stuck at the top of a tall mountain.

Noah opened a window to look out. The water was going down, but the world was far from dry.

So he sent out a dove. And when the dove did not come back, Noah knew that it had found a dry place to build its nest.

"Come out!" God called finally. "Come out of the boat! The world is dry. The world is ready for a fresh start. And now you and your family and all the animals must have children and fill it full of life again!"

"Hooray!" Noah celebrated. And he thanked God for saving him and his family.

God was happy too. So he painted the world's first rainbow in the sky – to celebrate his fresh, new world. And to promise that he would never send a flood like that again.

 Talk about a time you wanted to "start all over again". Was it because of something you did wrong or something someone did to you? Was it with a friend, maybe, or someone in your family? Was it at school, at home, at work?

 Perhaps the hardest part of this story to understand is God's decision to allow the rain waters above and the flood waters below to drown every living thing on the earth. Why do you think he did that? And why is what he did for Noah and his family and the animals on the ark so important?

 Doing a good thing was hard for Noah. Is doing good always hard?

 What are the USes in this story? How does putting ME first play a part?

List any other promises you know that God made to someone in the Bible. Did those promises come true?

 You could thank God for keeping his promises. You could ask for his help when you have to do something that is both good and hard.

19

God's Friend

Hi! My name is Abraham. This is the story of how God promised to make me the father of a great nation, even though I didn't have any children! If you want to read the story in the Bible, you can find it in Genesis, chapters 12 to 21.

Every time the story says, "Abraham trusted God," put your hand on your heart and repeat that line – "Abraham trusted God."

Abraham was rich. He had lots of servants to do his work for him. He had lots of camels and sheep. And he lived in a very nice place called Harran.

One day, God spoke to Abraham.

"I want you to leave Harran," he said. "I want to lead you to a better place. And I want to bless you with a family that will grow and grow and be a blessing to the world."

Now, Abraham might have said something like, "Where?" or "How far?" or "Thank you very much, but I'm quite happy here." But he didn't. In fact, he said nothing at all. He just gathered up his wife and his servants and his camels and his sheep, and went where God led him.

What questions about God's plan might you have asked God if you were me? Talk about a time when you had to trust God to help you do something, or trust in a promise he made.

Why? Because Abraham trusted God. It was as simple as that. Canaan was the name of the place where God led Abraham. And a very nice place it was. "A land flowing with milk and honey" is what some people called it. Which means that there were many cows and goats and bees there, and plenty of flowers and grass for the animals to eat. It was altogether a pretty place. And Abraham liked it very much.

> What is the nicest place you have ever lived? Or visited? Is there anywhere you would like to move to? What if God asked you to go to a place that wasn't very nice?

The only problem was that Abraham had no children. And besides that, both he and his wife, Sarah, were very old. Grandpa- and grandma-old, and maybe even older than that.

But Abraham trusted God. So one night God said to him, "Abraham, look up. Do you see the stars? One day you will have so many children and grandchildren and great-grandchildren that counting the stars will be an easy job compared with counting them."

What did Abraham do? Abraham trusted God, that's what. Even though God's promise seemed impossible.

"You will, indeed, have a son," God promised. "And through your family, I will do something wonderful for the world!"

So Abraham trusted God, and it wasn't long before God sent three messengers to visit him. Abraham was very kind to them. He washed their feet, which was the polite thing to do in those days. Then he served them fresh baked bread and a creamy beef stew. It was delicious! And as the visitors were patting their tummies and wiping their mouths, they said, "We will be back next year, and when we return, Sarah will give birth to a son!"

Someone giggled. Someone chuckled. Someone laughed. It was Sarah, who had been listening in the tent nearby! The whole idea seemed impossible. "Will I really have a child?" she wondered.

"Why did Sarah laugh?" the visitors asked. "Don't you know that God can do anything?"

So Abraham trusted God. And Sarah did too.

We were very old when God promised us a family. Draw a picture of someone a lot older than you. Your own grandpa or grandma, maybe. What would you say if you found out they were going to have a baby?

And, the next year, when God's promise came true and the baby was born, there was laughter again. So much laughter, in fact, that "Laughter" is what they decided to call their son. For that is what the name "Isaac" means.

 What do you find hard to trust God for? What do you find easy?

Has God ever done anything that made you laugh?

 Why do you think God chose Abraham?

 Can you list the USes in this story – the relationships? Might putting ME first have crept into this story anywhere? Here's a thought: is it possible that putting US first is also the best thing for ME? Talk about how that might have been true in Abraham's case.

 Pray that God will help you to trust him. To trust what he does. And to trust that what he says is true.

The Runaway

Hi! My name is Jacob. Abraham's son, Isaac, was my father. So Abraham was my grandpa. I had a twin brother too, called Esau, whom I cheated. If you want to find out how I cheated my brother, read Genesis, chapter 27. You might also like to read Genesis 25:29–34 to find out why I thought he might not care. In the end, Esau was so angry he wanted to kill me. But God was watching. And he had something very different in mind.

 Jacob ran.

Jacob ran and ran.

Jacob had cheated his brother, Esau. And now his brother wanted to kill him. So Jacob ran.

God watched.

God watched and watched.

God watched Jacob run. And when Jacob was tired and could run no further, when Jacob fell exhausted on the desert floor with only a stone for a pillow, when Jacob was finally ready to listen, God spoke.

He came to Jacob in a dream. There was a ladder, reaching right up to heaven, with angels parading up and down. And at the very top of the ladder stood God himself!

 Think of a time when you felt confident that God was watching over you.

"Jacob," he said. "I am the God of your father, Isaac, and your grandfather Abraham. And I am here to make you the same promise I made to them.

"This land is yours. Your family will be great. And one day, through your family, I will do something wonderful for the whole world! Now, go and don't be afraid, for you can always count on me to protect you."

Jacob woke up, amazed. He said "thank you" to God and he left a stone to mark that special place.

God told me that my family would do something wonderful for the world. He said the same thing to my father, Isaac, and my grandfather Abraham. I never lived to see it. Can you tell me what it is?

Then Jacob ran.

He ran and ran – all the way to his uncle Laban's house, where his mother had told him he would be safe. And where God knew he would learn an important lesson.

Now Laban had two daughters.

The older daughter's name was Leah – which means "Tired".

The younger daughter's name was Rachel – which means "Lamb".

Rachel was beautiful. And the moment Jacob set eyes on her, he knew she was the girl for him!

"Wonderful!" said Uncle Laban. "Work for me for seven years, and she will be your wife."

Seven years passed, but Jacob was so in love with Rachel that it seemed no longer than a day.

The wedding was well attended. The dress was beautiful. But when Jacob pulled aside the veil that hid his bride's face, he found himself looking into Leah's tired eyes!

"Oh, I forgot to mention," grinned Laban. "Leah is my eldest daughter, so she has to marry first. But you can marry Rachel, next week if you like, as long as you promise to work for me for another seven years."

Jacob looked at the ground. Now the cheater knew how it felt to be cheated.

Can you think of a time when something bad you did to someone else happened to you as well? What was the difference in how you felt after each? God talks about forgiveness and mercy and grace instead. Is there anything we can learn when we are hurt in the same way in which we have hurt someone else?

What else could Jacob do? He waited a week, married Rachel, and worked another seven years for Uncle Laban. Then he headed home, a very different man from the one who had run away.

Jacob walked and walked. And when his home was no more than a day's walk away, he saw Esau, his brother, walking toward him.

Jacob told his family to stay behind, and walked ahead to face his brother's anger. He wasn't running now. He believed that God would protect him.

And so God did – because Esau was different too. When he saw Jacob, he ran up to him, reached out his hairy arms, and hugged him!

"I'm sorry," said Jacob.

"I forgive you," Esau answered.

And the two sons of Isaac became brothers at last.

 Talk about a time when forgiving someone or being forgiven by someone made a difference in your life. Why is forgiveness better than "getting even"?

 Jacob does not seem to have been a very nice person. Why do you think God chose him to carry on the blessing that would one day bless the world?

 Can you list the relationships in this story? How did ME make a MEss of things? And what was it about US that made things better?

 You could pray that God will help you to forgive someone you struggle to forgive, and that he will help you to ask forgiveness from those you have hurt.

Joseph the Dreamer

Hi! My name is Joseph. Jacob was my dad and he treated me differently than he treated my brothers. This caused a lot of trouble. Trouble that God used to save our whole family! If you want to read my story in the Bible, you can find it in Genesis, chapters 37 to 45.

You might like to groan when the brothers do, and bow down in the dreams with them.

Jacob had twelve sons. That's right – twelve!

His favourite son was Joseph. Jacob spoiled him and gave him special gifts – like a beautiful coat decorated with many colours.

Reds and greens. Blues and yellows. Purples and pinks. Joseph was bright as a rainbow and proud as a peacock.

My dad liked me best of all! Do you think that parents should have favourites? What might go wrong if they do? How would you feel if you were the favourite? How would you feel if you weren't?

Joseph's older brothers did not like this one bit. But what they hated even more were Joseph's dreams!

"I had a dream last night," boasted Joseph.

"Oh no," groaned his brothers.

"I dreamed that we were all bundles of wheat. And guess what happened? Your bundles of wheat bowed down and worshipped mine!

"And I had another dream," Joseph bragged.

"Go on," his brothers sighed.

"I dreamed we were all stars. And guess what?

28

Your stars bowed down to mine, just as if I were your king!"

It didn't take long for Joseph's brothers to grow tired of this. But that's no excuse for what they did.

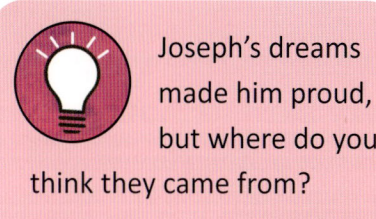
Joseph's dreams made him proud, but where do you think they came from?

The next time they were out of Jacob's sight, they grabbed Joseph, tore off his colourful coat, and dropped him down a dry well. They were just about to kill him, in fact,

Our brother really annoyed us. Do you have a brother or sister who annoys you? Why do they annoy you? What do you think the best way of dealing with that is? (Hint – following our example would be a bad idea.)

when they spotted a cloud of dust at the edge of the hill. It was a band of traders bound for Egypt, their camels loaded with goods for sale.

"Why should we kill Joseph," asked one of the brothers, "when we can sell him to these traders and make some money for ourselves? He'll be sold as a slave in Egypt and his foolish dreams will never come true!"

Twenty pieces of silver. That's how much the traders gave them for Joseph. And when the traders had gone, the brothers ripped up Joseph's coat, dipped it in the blood of a goat, and carried it home to their father.

"Joseph is dead," they told Jacob. And they showed him Joseph's coat, its long sleeves shredded, its beautiful colours smeared with blood.

Jacob wept and wept.

And Joseph wept too, as the traders carried him far from home.

Joseph's brothers sold Joseph for twenty pieces of silver. Do you know of anyone else in the Bible who was "sold" for pieces of silver?

Have you ever seen God use a bad thing that happened to bring about something good? Can you think of an example perhaps from the Bible, or maybe from your own experience or the experience of someone you know?

When the traders took Joseph to Egypt, they sold him to one of the king's own soldiers – a man named Potiphar. He was kind, and Joseph worked very hard for him. So hard, in fact, that Potiphar put Joseph in charge of all his other slaves.

Potiphar's wife, however, was evil and cruel. She tried to kiss Joseph, and when he wouldn't do it, she told lies about Joseph and had him thrown in prison!

Things looked bad for Joseph. It seemed as if his dreams would never come true. But God was watching over him.

Why do you think Potiphar's wife told lies about me? How do you think I felt when she told these lies? And how do you think I felt when Potiphar believed her? Has anyone ever told lies about you? How did that feel?

When Joseph was thrown into prison, do you think he might have thought that God had forgotten him? What did God do to show him that he was still there?

One morning, one of the other prisoners said, "I had a dream last night. A strange dream. I dreamed I saw a grapevine with three branches. Suddenly, bunches of grapes burst out of those branches. So I squeezed them into a cup and gave it to the king to drink. I wonder what it means?"

Joseph listened to the dream. God listened too. Then he whispered the dream's meaning into Joseph's ear.

"I know what it means!" said Joseph. "Before you were sent to prison, you served wine to the king. Well, in three days, you will be set free and serve him wine once more."

That's exactly what happened. And when the wine-server was set free, he promised to help Joseph get out too.

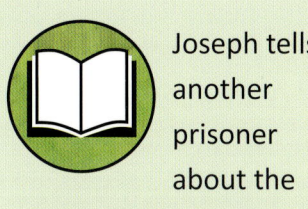
Joseph tells another prisoner about the meaning of a dream, but there wasn't room for it here. It doesn't have a very happy ending, but you can read about it in Genesis, chapter 40.

Two long years went by. Then, one morning, the king of Egypt said, "I had a dream last night. A strange dream! And I can't work out what it means."

"A dream?" said his wine-server. "I know a man who can tell you all about your dreams."

And straight away Joseph was brought from the prison.

"I was standing on the banks of the river," the king told Joseph, "when I saw seven fat cows walk up out of the water. They were chewing happily on the grass when seven other cows joined them. These cows were bony and thin and, instead of eating the grass, they ate the first seven cows. But they stayed as skinny as ever! What can it mean?"

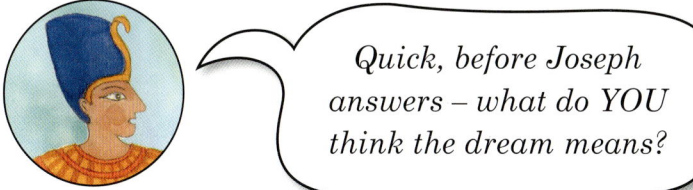
Quick, before Joseph answers – what do YOU think the dream means?

God whispered in Joseph's ear. Joseph listened. Then he bowed and said, "Your Majesty, for the next seven years Egypt will grow many good crops and be as fat as those first cows. But after that, for another seven years, hardly any food at all will grow. So unless you want your people to look like those skinny cows, you must store up food in the good years and use it wisely later."

The king was so impressed with Joseph's answer that he not only let him stay out of prison, he put him in charge of storing and saving and serving out Egypt's food.

Seven good years *were* followed by seven bad. And, after the king, Joseph became the most important man in Egypt. It was like a dream come true!

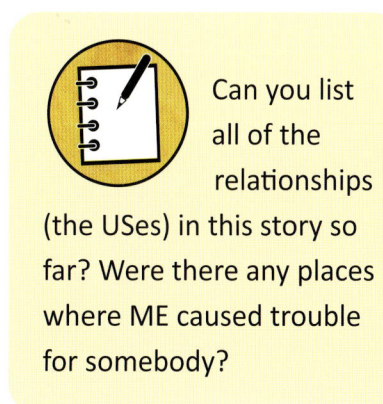
Can you list all of the relationships (the USes) in this story so far? Were there any places where ME caused trouble for somebody?

31

One day there was a knock at Joseph's door. And when he answered it, his eleven brothers were standing there!

They bowed down before him. They kissed his feet. And they begged, "Kind sir, we have come to Egypt all the way from the land of Canaan. We have no food. We are starving. May we please buy some from you?"

Joseph said nothing. He just stared at his brothers. He knew who they were, but they did not recognize him.

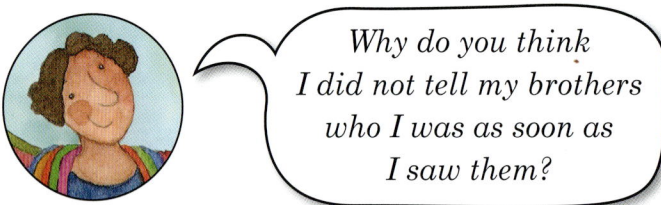

Why do you think I did not tell my brothers who I was as soon as I saw them?

"All right," said Joseph, in his sternest voice. "I will sell you food." And he ordered his servants to load his brothers' animals.

But that wasn't all he told them to do. "Take one of my silver cups," he said, "and hide it in the sack of food tied to the donkey of Benjamin, the youngest brother." Joseph had a plan. He wanted to see if his brothers had changed.

When Joseph's brothers reached the edge of the city, his servants stopped them and searched through their sacks. What did they find? The silver cup, of course!

"We don't know how it got there!" the brothers exclaimed to Joseph.

"Your brother stole it, that's how," Joseph answered. "So he must stay here in Egypt and be my slave."

"No, please," begged the brothers. "That would break our father's heart. Keep one of us instead."

How did I know that my brothers had changed? How did that have anything to do with what they had done to me all those years before?

When Joseph heard that, he knew his brothers had changed. So he told them who he was, right then and there.

"I am Joseph," he announced, "your long-lost brother."

This news did not make his brothers feel any better. They were so frightened, in fact, that they could hardly speak.

Why do you think we were frightened when Joseph told us who he was?

"Don't be afraid," said Joseph, "I forgive you. You meant to hurt me, but God used what you did to save us all from this terrible famine. Now, go. Fetch my father and the rest of our family to come and live in Egypt with me."

The brothers looked up.
The brothers grinned.
The brothers cheered!
And after a lot of hugging and hello-ing and handshaking, they set off for Canaan to tell Jacob the good news.

How do you think I reacted when I heard that my son Joseph was alive?

And Joseph? Joseph just sat back on his throne and smiled. And thanked God for making his dreams come true.

 List all of the things that God did to turn the bad thing the brothers had done into something good.

How is this story a good example of the way that ME can be turned into US?

 What was it exactly that God was trying to "save" through what he did in this story?

 You could give God thanks for everyone in your family. Ask him to help when you fall out with each other.

The Great Escape

Hi! My name is Moses. It's a name that means "drawn out" or "pulled out". My mother called me that. Well, not my real mother, who was one of the descendants of Joseph, but the mother who raised me, who was an Egyptian princess! It's complicated, really (you can read the story in Exodus, chapters 1 and 2). Let's just say that more than a hundred years after Joseph more or less saved the Egyptians, a pharaoh came along who didn't remember what Joseph had done and was frightened by the huge number of Joseph's descendants. So he turned them into slaves. God decided to do something about that, and that is where I came into the picture…

The sun was burning hot. Moses' skin was burned dark brown.

And suddenly, he saw it – a bright red burning bush!

Its branches crackled orange and red, and Moses could not help but watch – for the bush did not burn up!

"Take off your shoes," came a voice from the bush. "This is a very special place."

What would you think if you saw a bush that was on fire but didn't burn up? What would you do? And how would you react if a voice came out of the bush?

"Who are you?" asked Moses. "And why are you talking to me? I am just a poor shepherd."

"I am the God of Abraham, Isaac, and Jacob," the voice replied. "And you are more than a shepherd. You are Moses, the man I have chosen to lead my people, the Israelites, out of Egypt."

"I can't do that," Moses trembled. "I left Egypt years ago, because I killed somebody. And I'm an old man now."

"You can do it. You must do it," God answered, "for my people are slaves in Egypt and have prayed to be set free. I have heard their prayers, and you are the man I have chosen."

Why do you think God chose me? Do you think it had anything to do with who my mother was, or how I was raised? You might find some answers in Exodus, chapter 3.

I was king of one of the biggest superpowers in my world. And God asked Moses, a nobody as I saw him, to challenge me. How do you think you would react if God asked you to challenge one of the superpowers in your time?

God heard the cries of his people – his people who were slaves. What kind of people are crying out in the world today for God to save them? What might we be able to do to help them?

It started almost at once. The rivers of Egypt filled with blood. The houses of Egypt swarmed with frogs. The dust of Egypt turned into gnats.

But the king would not let God's people go.

The people in Egypt were covered with flies. The animals in Egypt grew sick and died. And ugly sores broke out on everyone.

But still the king would not let God's people go.

Hail pelted the land and broke down the crops. Locusts gobbled up what was left. Then darkness like night fell for three whole days.

And still the king would not give in.

Finally, God sent an angel to kill the king's eldest son. And the eldest sons of the rest of the Egyptians.

Then, at last, the king said, "Go! Go, and never come back!"

> If you had been an Egyptian at that time, how would these plagues have affected you? How would they have changed your life?

> Why do you think it was this plague that made me finally change my mind? Why do you think I changed my mind back again and chased after the Israelites?

God's people cheered. God's people packed. God's people waved goodbye. But just as they reached the sea and were puzzling out how to get across, the king changed his mind!

He leaped into his chariot and led his army out after them. Soon, the sea stretched out before God's people and the Egyptian army rushed behind them like a wave. What could they do?

"Raise your special walking stick," God whispered to Moses. And the sea split in two before them – leaving a path right down the middle! The people of Israel hurried along that path to the other side, the Egyptian army close behind. Just as the last of God's people had safely crossed, Moses lowered his stick, the waters rushed back, and the army was washed away.

God's people were free at last!

Try to describe how it would feel if you were a slave. Then try to describe how it would feel if you had suddenly been set free.

As the people faced the Red Sea roaring ahead of them with the army of Egypt roaring up behind, what do you think went through the minds of God's people?

What are the relationships in this story? Where are they positive and good? Where do they struggle? Is there anyone in the story who is focused mostly on ME?

You could pray for the millions of people who are still trapped in slavery around the world.

The Walls Fall Down

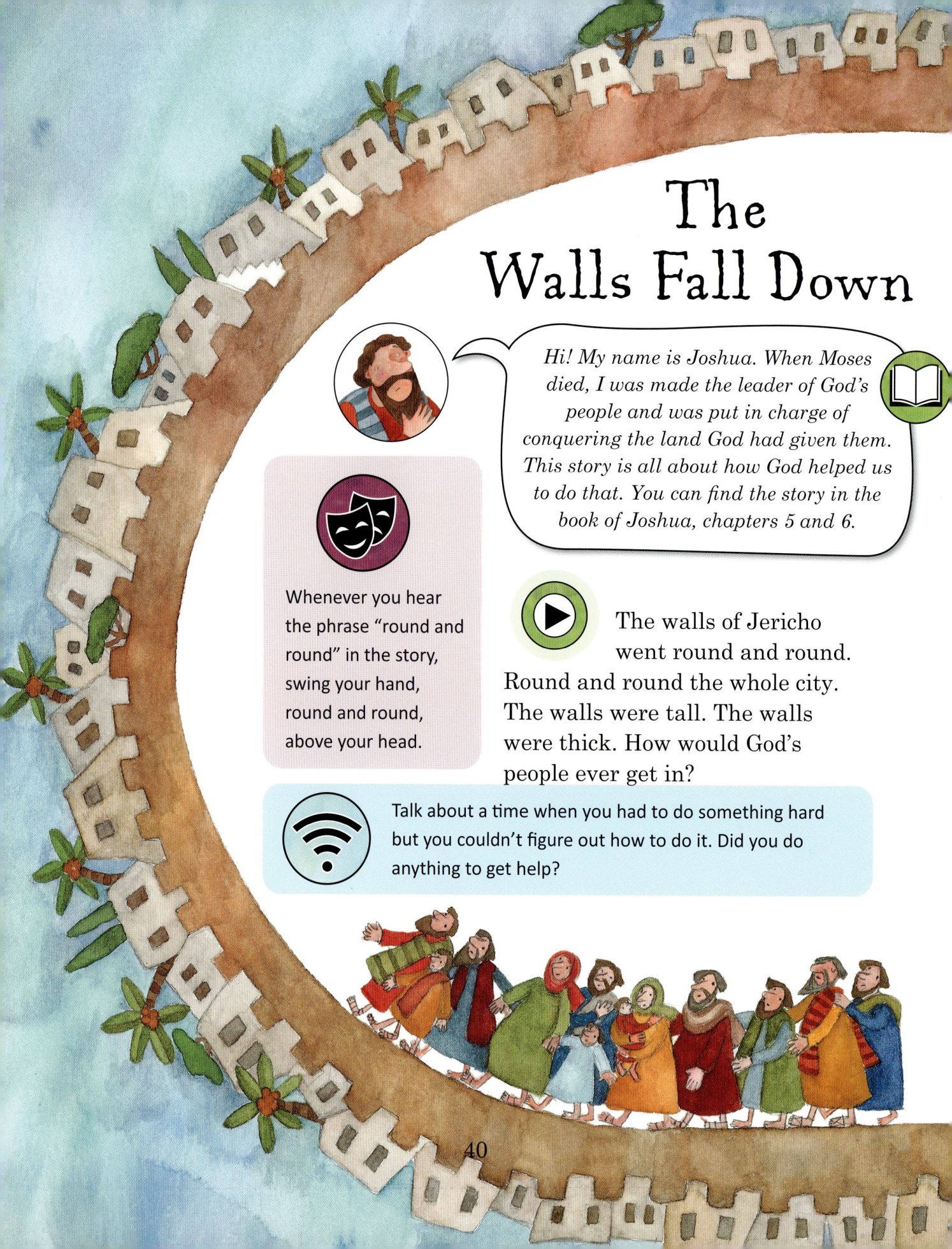

Hi! My name is Joshua. When Moses died, I was made the leader of God's people and was put in charge of conquering the land God had given them. This story is all about how God helped us to do that. You can find the story in the book of Joshua, chapters 5 and 6.

Whenever you hear the phrase "round and round" in the story, swing your hand, round and round, above your head.

The walls of Jericho went round and round. Round and round the whole city. The walls were tall. The walls were thick. How would God's people ever get in?

Talk about a time when you had to do something hard but you couldn't figure out how to do it. Did you do anything to get help?

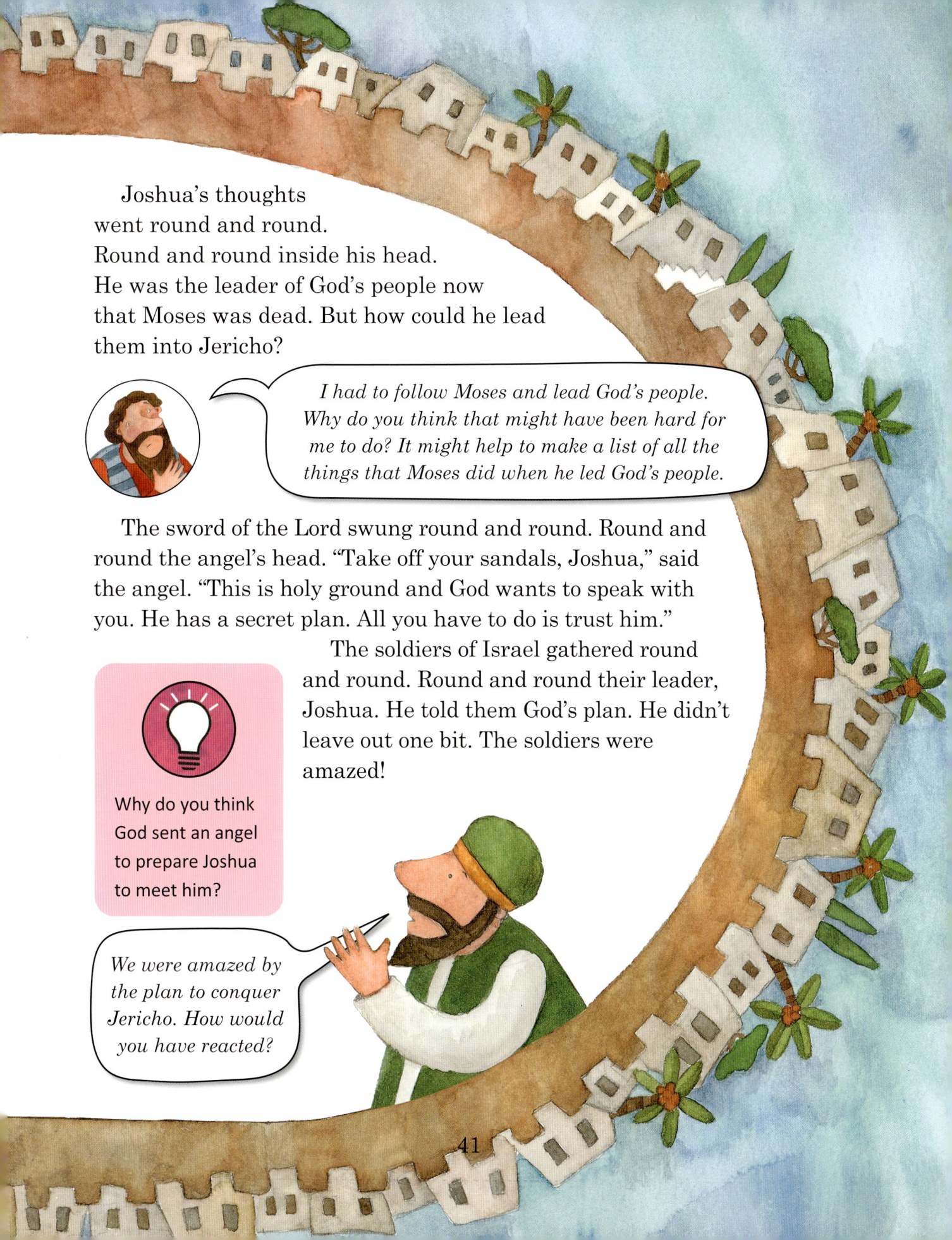

Joshua's thoughts went round and round. Round and round inside his head. He was the leader of God's people now that Moses was dead. But how could he lead them into Jericho?

I had to follow Moses and lead God's people. Why do you think that might have been hard for me to do? It might help to make a list of all the things that Moses did when he led God's people.

The sword of the Lord swung round and round. Round and round the angel's head. "Take off your sandals, Joshua," said the angel. "This is holy ground and God wants to speak with you. He has a secret plan. All you have to do is trust him."

The soldiers of Israel gathered round and round. Round and round their leader, Joshua. He told them God's plan. He didn't leave out one bit. The soldiers were amazed!

Why do you think God sent an angel to prepare Joshua to meet him?

We were amazed by the plan to conquer Jericho. How would you have reacted?

So the army of Israel marched round and round. Round and round the walls of Jericho. Once round each day. Six days in a row. And the people of Jericho laughed.

"Why are they marching round and round? Round and round the walls of Jericho? Is this a parade? Is it some kind of trick? They'll never beat us this way!"

But when the army marched round and round, round and round on the seventh day – they marched round once, they marched round twice. They marched round Jericho seven times. Then they raised their voices. They blew their trumpets. And the walls came crashing down!

How does it feel when people laugh at you and make fun of you?

The people of Israel danced round and round. Round and round the ruins of Jericho. "God is our helper!" they sang and they shouted. "He will never let us down!"

The people were very grateful when God did not let them down. Talk about a time when you were grateful that God did not let you down, or were disappointed when you thought he had.

The people of Jericho were amused by what the Israelites were doing. Can you think of any other place in the Bible where someone was laughed at because people did not understand what they were doing? Has that ever happened to you?

What are the important relationships in this story? List them.

Maybe you are faced with doing something hard. You could pray for God's help in this situation.

A Brave and Mighty Man

Hi! My name is Gideon. Once God's people had conquered and settled in the land God promised to give them, they were supposed to live the way he wanted them to live. Whenever they stopped doing that, though, their enemies would fight them and sometimes even rule over them. So God would give his Holy Spirit to men and women called judges, to lead the fight against those enemies. Samson, Deborah, Ehud, and others were in that list of judges. And so was I!

"Gideon," the angel whispered. "Oh, Gideon," the angel called. "Your people need your help, you brave and mighty man."

But Gideon was hiding – in a pit his father used for crushing grapes.

"You can't be talking to me," Gideon stammered. "I'm no brave and mighty man."

But God knew what he was doing. He always does.

> Why do you think the angel called Gideon a brave and mighty man when he was hiding from his enemies?

"You're the man all right," the angel explained. "The Midianites are crushing God's people, destroying their crops and killing their animals. And he wants you to round up an army to stop them!"

Gideon did what the angel told him. And, to his surprise, over 30,000 men agreed to join him!

"Gideon," God whispered. "Oh, Gideon," God called. "You have far too many men in your army. I want you to send some of them away."

How do you think I felt when God told me to send some of my army away?

"There are more Midianites than I can count!" Gideon stammered. "I need all the help I can get."

But God knew what he was doing. He always does.

"I am all the help you need," God said. "So tell the men who are frightened to go home."

Gideon did what God told him. And when he had finished, there were only 10,000 left.

"Gideon," God whispered. "Oh, Gideon," God called. "You still have too many men. So here's what I want you to do…"

Gideon listened to God's plan. Gideon stammered and shook. Then he led his men to the river and told them to have a drink.

Some soldiers knelt down and drank straight from the river; Gideon sent them home.

Others scooped up the water in their hands. Those were the soldiers Gideon kept. And when he had finished, there were only 300 left!

What was the difference in the way the soldiers drank the water? Do you think that had anything to do with why some of them were kept and some were sent home? Why?

Are there things that Christians do that people who are not Christians find strange? If so, can you list some of them?

"Gideon," God whispered. "Oh, Gideon," God called.
"Now we are ready to fight the Midianites."

"But there are thousands of them," Gideon stammered.
"And only 300 of us. How can we possibly win?"

"You can't," God said. "Not without my help. And that's what I want you to see. Here's my plan…"

How do you think I felt just before I explained God's plan to my soldiers? What do think their reaction was when they heard it?

Talk about a time when someone else saw something about you that you didn't see in yourself. How did that affect you?

Later that night, Gideon led his 300 men to the edge of the Midianite camp. In one hand every soldier carried a trumpet and in the other hand a clay pot with a flaming torch inside. There wasn't a sword in sight! At Gideon's signal, the soldiers blew their trumpets, smashed their pots, and shouted, "For the Lord and for Gideon!"

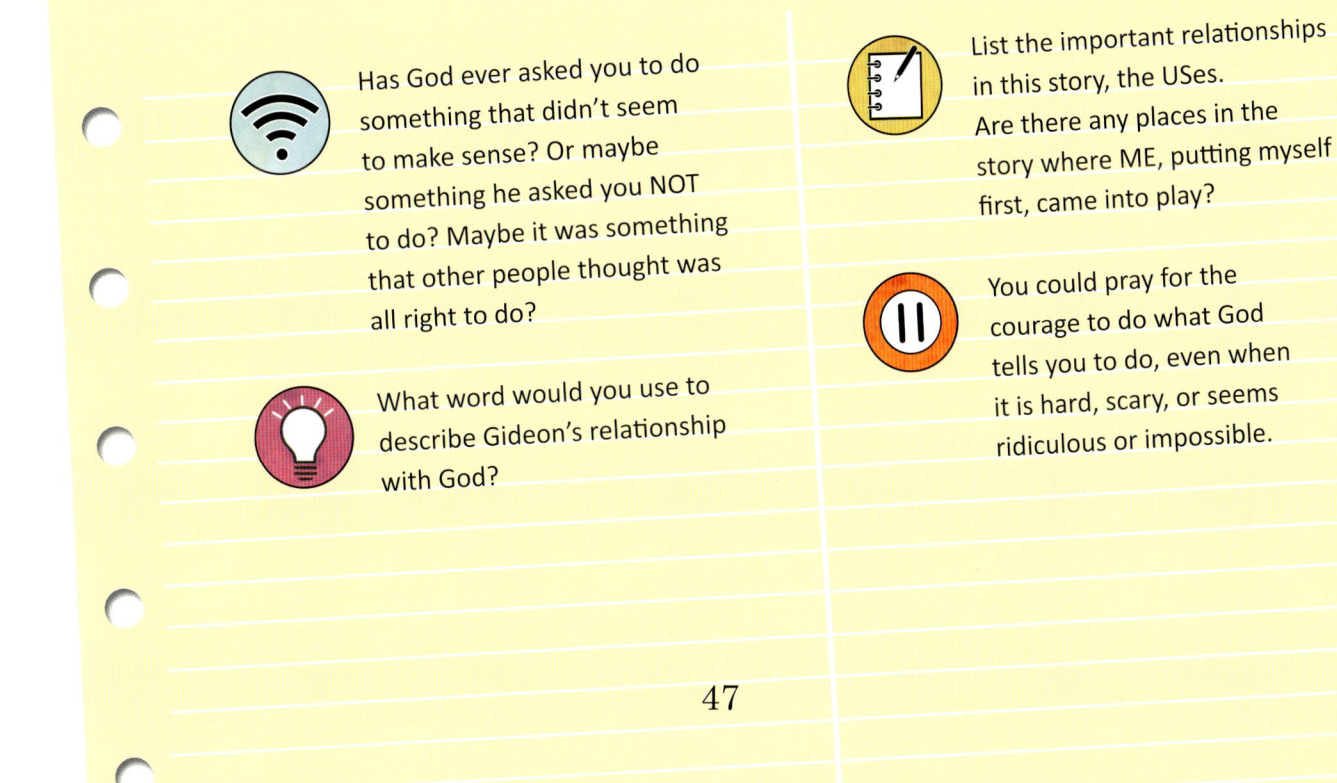

The Midianite soldiers awoke, startled.

It seemed as if there was noise and fire all around them! Dazed and confused, they stumbled about in the dark – into each other and over each other. And it wasn't long before they were fighting each other too!

When all the fighting had stopped, the Midianite soldiers who were left ran away, convinced that they had been defeated by some great army. But it was only Gideon, his 300 men, and a God who knew what he was doing all along.

Has God ever asked you to do something that didn't seem to make sense? Or maybe something he asked you NOT to do? Maybe it was something that other people thought was all right to do?

What word would you use to describe Gideon's relationship with God?

List the important relationships in this story, the USes. Are there any places in the story where ME, putting myself first, came into play?

You could pray for the courage to do what God tells you to do, even when it is hard, scary, or seems ridiculous or impossible.

Ruth Finds a New Home

Hi! My name is Ruth. My story took place near the end of the time of the judges. Unlike many of the people you will read about in the Bible, I wasn't even an Israelite. I came to live in the land of Israel from another country entirely. Why I was there, and what happened to me after I arrived, and how God made my story a part of his Great Big Story, can be found in the book of Ruth. And you can read a version of that story here.

Naomi was lonely. Her husband was dead. So were her two sons. And she was living in a country that was far from home with her sons' widows, Orpah and Ruth.

"I'm going home," said Naomi to her daughters-in-law one day. "Back to my own country. Back to Bethlehem, where I belong. You must stay here. I will miss you, but this is your country, not mine."

Naomi expected Orpah and Ruth to kiss her and hug her and wave goodbye. And that is just what Orpah did. But Ruth did something different.

She kissed Naomi, and she hugged Naomi, and then she said, "I'm coming with you."

"Why?" asked Naomi. "Why leave your people and your home to travel to a place you do

Naomi was sad and lonely because her husband and sons had died. Talk about a time when you felt sad or lonely because someone you cared about was gone. What did you do?

Why do you think Orpah chose to stay and Ruth chose to follow Naomi to her homeland? Is there someone you care for whom you would follow anywhere?

not know? Here you have a chance of finding another husband. But I can't give you one."

But no matter what Naomi said, Ruth would not change her mind. She cared for Naomi and wanted to make sure that she returned home safe and sound.

"I'm going with you," she said. "And that's all there is to it. From now on, your people will be my people and your God will be my God."

Why do you think I told Naomi that her people would be my people? And why do you think I told her that her God would be my God? Was there any connection between her God and her people?

So Naomi and Ruth went to Bethlehem. And while Naomi greeted her relatives, Ruth went off to find a job. That was hard, however, because she came from a different country. So she ended up gathering bits of barley in a field that belonged to a man named Boaz – bits that were left behind when the workers collected the grain.

Have you ever gone to a new place – school, job, club, city, country – where you felt like you didn't belong? How did that affect you? Did you ever want to just leave and go back to where you had come from?

Boaz soon noticed Ruth. He had heard about what she'd done for Naomi. He admired her courage and her loyalty. And he also took a shine to her. And that is why the next day he told his workers that they should leave a bit more barley behind, on purpose. Now Ruth would have more to take home with her.

> Talk about a time when you did something kind for an outsider, someone who didn't feel like they belonged. Or talk about a time when someone did that for you.

Ruth was delighted. And when she told Naomi what had happened, and when she showed Naomi all the barley she'd found, Naomi asked her who the field belonged to.

"A man named Boaz," said Ruth.

And now Naomi was delighted too. Because Boaz was one of her relatives! And in a flash, Naomi turned from mother-in-law to matchmaker.

"Put on your best dress," she told Ruth. "And a little perfume too. You're going to visit Boaz tonight!"

And so Ruth did. And Boaz liked her so much that he immediately arranged to marry her.

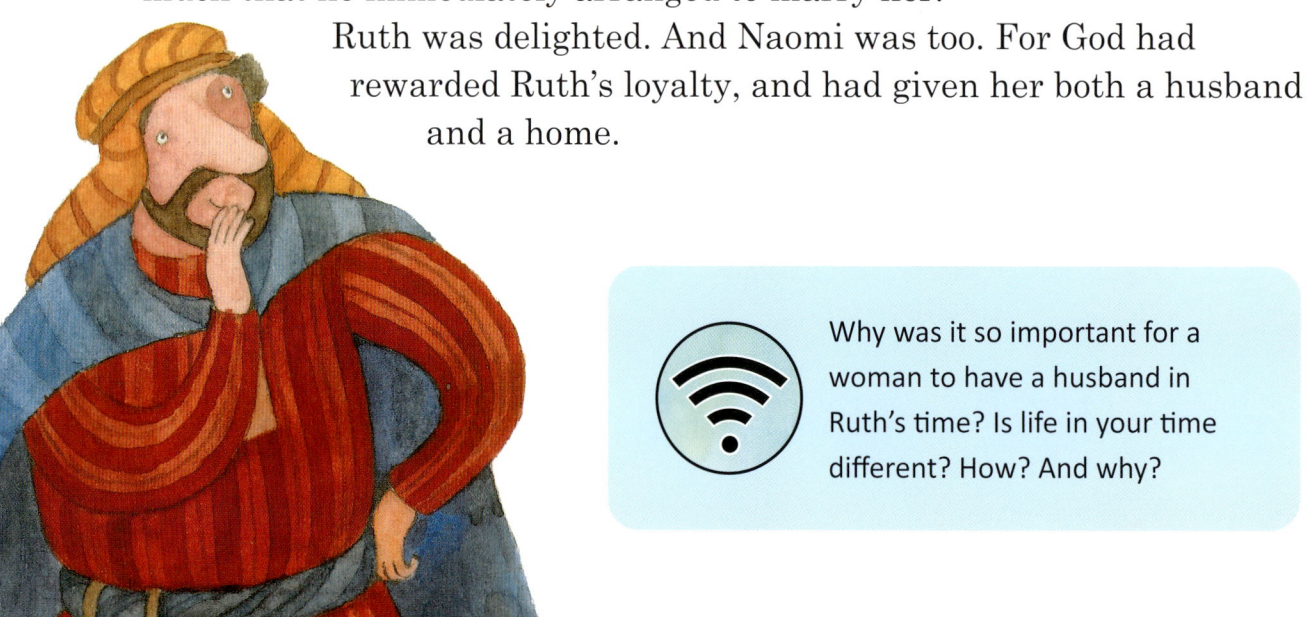

Ruth was delighted. And Naomi was too. For God had rewarded Ruth's loyalty, and had given her both a husband and a home.

> Why was it so important for a woman to have a husband in Ruth's time? Is life in your time different? How? And why?

And what is more, Ruth later gave birth to a son whose name was Obed. And Obed's son was Jesse. And one of Jesse's sons was a shepherd boy named David, who ran into a giant one day. But that's another story!

Ruth was an immigrant – a person who came from one country to live in a different one.
Are immigrants always welcome in the countries to which they go? How do you think God feels about immigrants?
Boaz showed kindness to Ruth. He let her gather extra grain. Is there any way that we can help immigrants in our time and place?

Think about a time when God brought good out of something bad that had happened.

What are the important relationships in this story? List all the USes. Did anyone put ME first and act selfishly?

You could pray for those who are forced by circumstances beyond their control to live in a foreign land.

"Samuel," God called again, "Samuel, listen."

Samuel was confused this time. And a little scared. So he crept back into Eli's room.

Why do you think Samuel was confused and scared the second time he heard the voice?

"I told you, boy," yawned the old priest. "I didn't call you. Now off to bed!"

Samuel didn't know what to think as he crawled under his covers. But when God called, "Samuel, Samuel," for the third time, he knew what to do.

He dashed back to Eli, just as fast as he could!

"Samuel," sighed Eli, "if either of us is going to get any sleep tonight, we need to find out who's calling you. And I have an idea who it might be. So, the next time you hear that voice, I don't want you to come running in here. Instead, I want you to say, 'Speak, Lord, and I will listen.'"

Was there ever a time in your life when you thought that God was speaking to you? What did you do?

Samuel's eyes opened wide. "You mean it's God who's calling me?"

"Do as I tell you," said Eli, "and we'll find out."

So Samuel went back to bed.

God called his name again.

This time Samuel stayed there and listened to God, and his eyes opened wide with wonder.

And from that moment until Samuel was himself an old man, God talked to Samuel, giving him messages to pass on to the people. And, just like the first time, God's messages never failed to leave him wide-eyed with wonder.

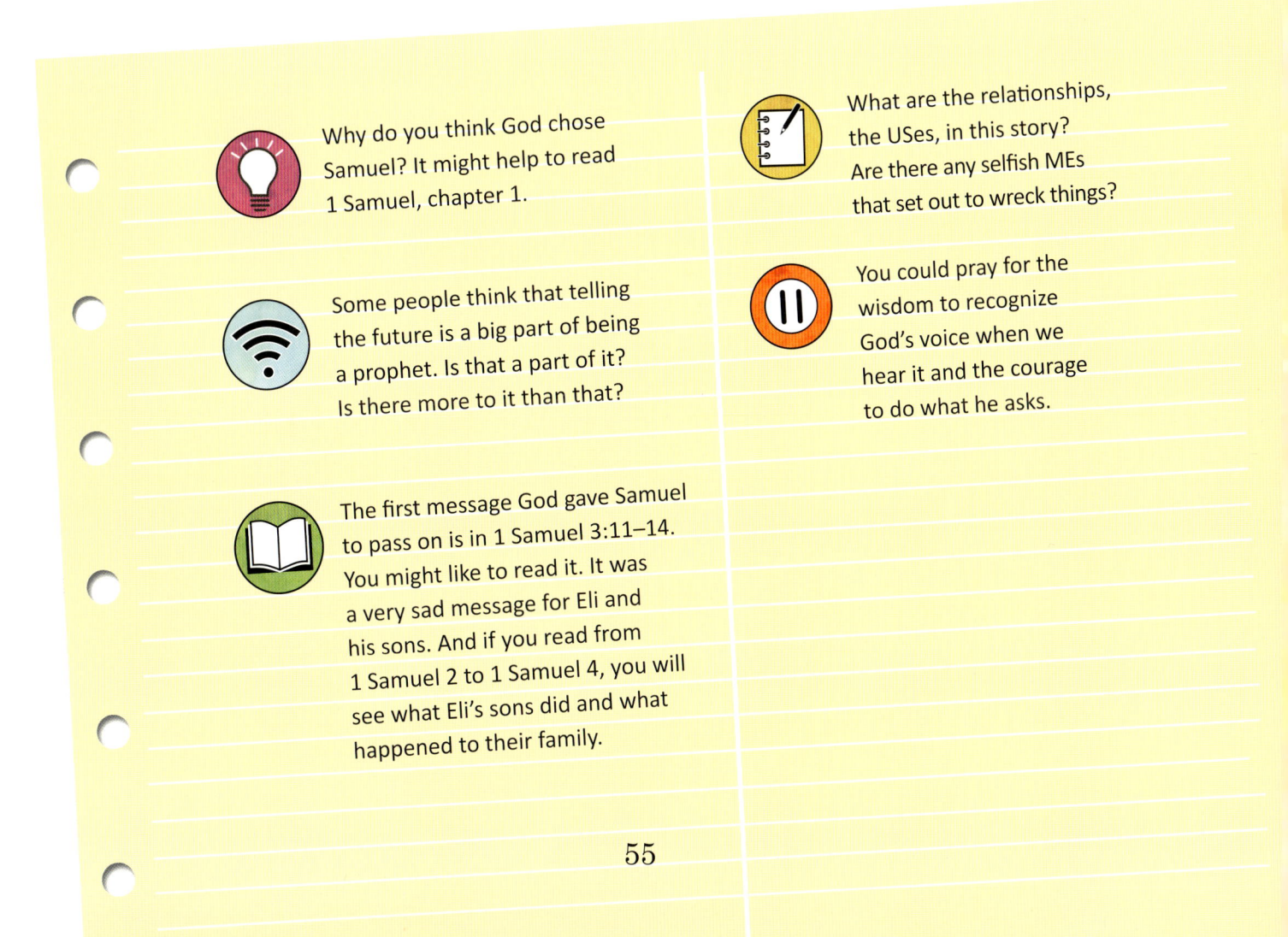

Why do you think God chose Samuel? It might help to read 1 Samuel, chapter 1.

Some people think that telling the future is a big part of being a prophet. Is that a part of it? Is there more to it than that?

The first message God gave Samuel to pass on is in 1 Samuel 3:11–14. You might like to read it. It was a very sad message for Eli and his sons. And if you read from 1 Samuel 2 to 1 Samuel 4, you will see what Eli's sons did and what happened to their family.

What are the relationships, the USes, in this story? Are there any selfish MEs that set out to wreck things?

You could pray for the wisdom to recognize God's voice when we hear it and the courage to do what he asks.

David the Giant-Killer

Hi! My name is David. I was the second king of Israel. The people of Israel were desperate for a king, so God allowed it (grudgingly) and his prophet Samuel anointed a man called Saul to be Israel's first king. He was tall and handsome. He looked like a king! But he was terrible really. And, in the end, Saul didn't listen to God or to Samuel. So God told Samuel to find another king, and Samuel came to my house. He looked at all my tall handsome brothers. And then God chose me! It had something to do with God looking at my heart and not my face. Which is a compliment (I guess). This is the story of one amazing thing God helped me do. You can find it in 1 Samuel, chapter 17.

Repeat Goliath's lines with a big roaring voice. And repeat David's lines with a little voice.

▶ Goliath was big.

He had to stoop to get through doorways. His head was always bumping up against the ceiling. And his friends thought twice before inviting him to dinner.

Goliath had a big spear. Three metres (ten feet) long, at least. With a big iron point. And his big bronze armour weighed sixty kilograms (a hundred pounds) or more.

Goliath had a big voice, too.

And, one day, he used it. He stamped out in front of his army, the Philistines, and shouted across the valley to the Israelite soldiers camped on the other side.

"I am Goliath!" he bellowed. "And I dare any of you to come and fight me. Win the fight, and we will be your slaves. Lose, and you must work for us."

How would you have reacted if you had been a soldier of Israel, had seen me, and had heard me shout my challenge?

David was little.

Just a boy, really, who looked after the sheep. When he wanted a break from that, he carried cheese to his brothers in the army. And that's what he was doing one day, when he heard Goliath shout.

David was a little angry.

"Who does that giant think he is?" huffed David. "Doesn't he know that the Lord God himself watches over us? Why, with God's help, even I could beat that bully."

Why do you think I was willing to fight the giant?

So David took a little walk. He went to see the king.

"I want to fight the giant," he announced.

And the king almost fell off his throne.

"But you are so little," said the king. "And he is so big!"

"A lion is big," answered David. "And so is a bear. But when they came after my sheep, the Lord God helped me face them and fight them off. He will do the same with this giant."

"All right," the king agreed. "But at least let me lend you my armour."

The armour was big. Too big. And so heavy that David could hardly move.

So he gave it back. And picked up five little stones instead. And a sling. And his trusty shepherd's staff.

Why do you think I gave the armour back to the king? Why did I decide to use stones and a sling instead?

Goliath gave a big laugh when he saw the little shepherd boy. And he took two big steps.

David ran a little way towards the giant.

Two more giant steps for Goliath.

And David ran a little further.

They were in the middle of the valley now, and everything was quiet.

> *Put yourself in our place. How do you think we felt when our little brother was in the middle of that field, facing the giant?*

Goliath roared a big roar, sucked in a big breath of air, and raised his big spear.

David sneaked his little hand into his little pouch, pulled out a little stone, and slipped it in his sling. Then he spun it around his head and let it fly.

And before the giant could say another word, the stone struck him on the head, and he fell with a big thud to the ground.

David's side shouted a big "Hooray!"

Goliath's side whispered, "Uh-oh."

And from then on, some pretty big things happened to the little shepherd boy. He was given a king's reward. He was promised the hand of the king's daughter in marriage. And, one day, he became king himself! The very best king God's people ever had.

Talk about a time when you had a "giant-sized" problem to deal with. Did you ask God for help in that situation? Did help come? How?

List the relationships in the story – all of the USes. Were any of those relationships helpful to David? Did any MEs cause problems? Sometimes putting US first brings out the best in ME. How did that happen in this story?

Pray for God's wisdom and courage and help with some giant-sized problem you or someone you know is facing.

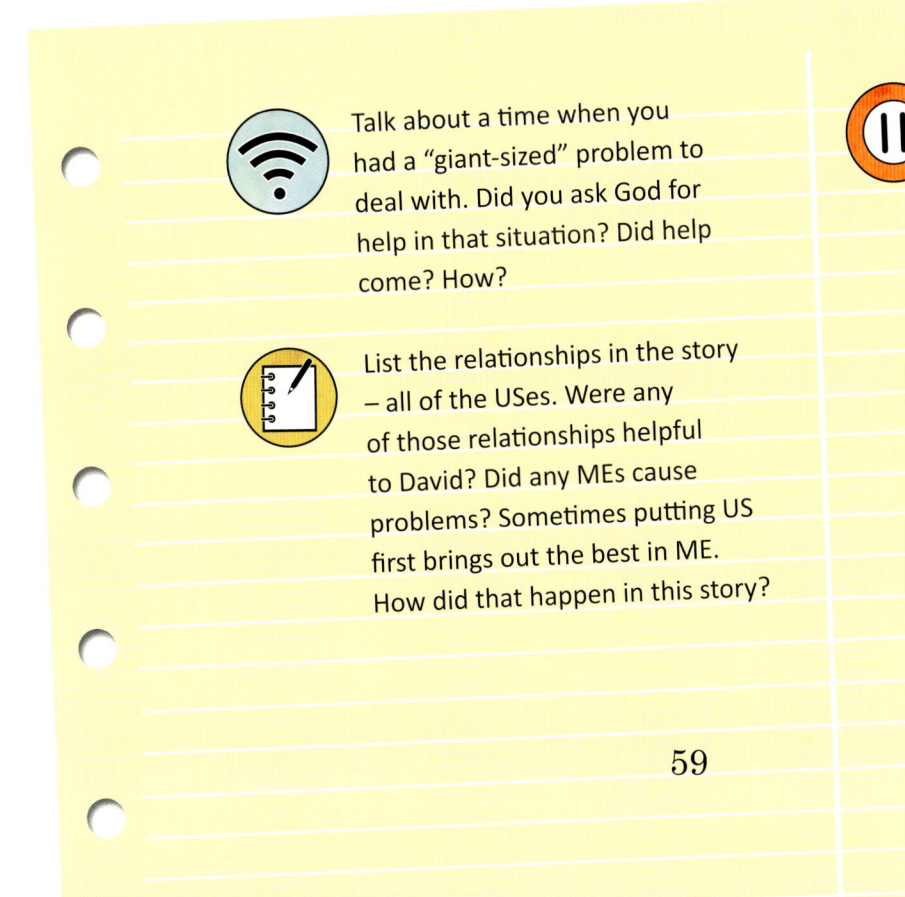

The Wise King

Hi! My name is Solomon. My father was King David. A lot of people wanted to take his place. There was even a rebellion, led by my brother Absalom. But that failed, and I became king of Israel instead. It was a big job, though. And I knew I needed God's help. This is the story of the very special thing God gave me. You can read about it yourself in 1 Kings, chapter 3.

As you read the story, repeat the "no", "not likely", "never" lines, shaking your head as you do.

When David died, his son Solomon became Israel's new king. And what do you think was the very first thing he did?

Pass some new law? No.

Send his army to fight some new enemy? Not likely.

Order himself a fancy new crown? Never.

No, the first thing he did was to kneel down before God and pray.

"Good for you!" God said to Solomon. "Now what would you like me to give you?"

Solomon could have prayed for anything. Anything at all! But what do you think he asked for?

A long life? No.

Victory in battle? Not likely.

Loads of money? Never.
No, the only thing he asked for was… wisdom!

I asked God to give me wisdom. Do you think that had anything to do with who my father was?

"It's going to be hard ruling over all these people," he prayed. "And I want to do the best job that I can. So help me, God. Give me wisdom to make the right choices and do the right things."

God was so pleased with Solomon's choice that he promised to give him wisdom – *and* all the other things, as well. A long life, victory, and loads of money!

Why do you think God gave me the other things as well, when all I asked for was wisdom?

How would you define wisdom if someone asked you what it was?

Can you think of a time when you weren't particularly wise – when you did something foolish?

It wasn't long before Solomon's wisdom was put to the test.

Two women came to see him one day. One of them was holding a baby. And the other one was very unhappy.

"That woman stole my baby!" she cried. "Her baby died. And while I was sleeping, she came and took mine!"

"That's a lie!" shouted the woman with the baby. And she held the child even more tightly.

Solomon looked at the women. Solomon looked at the baby. And what do you think he did?

Give the baby to the first woman? No.

Give the baby to the second woman? Not likely.

Keep it for himself? Never.

No, he called one of his soldiers and told him to raise his sword above the child.

How do you think I felt when the king asked me to raise my sword above the baby?

"Now cut the baby in half," Solomon ordered, "and each of the women can have a piece."

The soldier was shocked. He looked at the king. He looked at the baby. But before he could use his sword, the woman who claimed her child had been stolen cried, "Stop! Let her have the child. He's my baby, but I'd rather see him raised by another than have him cut in two."

"Oh no," said the woman holding the baby. "The king is right. Cut the baby in half!"

It was exactly what Solomon had hoped for.

"Now I see who the real mother is," he said. "She would rather give up her child than see it harmed." And he took the baby from one woman and gave it to the other.

Explain how Solomon used his wisdom in this story. Do you think he would really have made the soldier harm the baby?

And what do you think God's people did?
They clapped.
They cheered.
And they thanked God for giving them a king who was both wise and good.

Can you give an example of someone showing wisdom, from your own experience?

Sadly, Solomon did not always show wisdom in the way he acted. You might like to read 1 Kings 11 to see how things went wrong.

List the relationships in this story – the USes. How did Solomon's prayer reflect the importance of US? And how did the difference between US and ME show itself in the response of the two women?

You might want to pray that God would gift you with wisdom as well, particularly with any difficult and tricky situations you are facing.

God Sends Fire

Hi! My name is Elijah. King Solomon's reign started well. He even got to build the beautiful Temple in Jerusalem where God's people went to worship. But things went downhill from there. He married lots of foreign wives, and he worshipped their foreign gods as well. That made God angry, so he let Solomon's kingdom be divided in two. The southern kingdom was called Judah. They had one or two good kings. The northern kingdom was called Israel, and they had no good kings at all. Israel is where I lived. When God called me to be his prophet, he sent me to pass his message on to one of the worst kings of all, Ahab.

During the story you could act out the stacking of the wood ("grunt grunt grunt"), the killing of the bull ("Moo!" "Urp"), and the crazy dancing about of the prophets of Baal. Then act out the piling of the stones (twelve "thumps"), the stacking of the wood ("grunt grunt grunt"), the killing of the bull ("Moo!" "Urp"), and the prayer to God of Elijah.

If David was the best king God's people ever had, then Ahab was one of the worst! He didn't listen to the Lord God at all. No, he worshipped a statue called Baal. And what is worse, he made a lot of God's people do the same.

God was watching this, of course. And he was not happy that his people had forgotten him and had replaced him with a god who was nothing more than a pile of stones.

So God whispered into the ear of Elijah – a man who had not forgotten him.

"Elijah," God whispered, "tell King Ahab that what he is

Why do you think God was not happy that his people were worshipping a statue instead of him? What was the difference between God and that statue?

doing is wrong. Tell him that I will stop the rain from falling until he stops worshipping Baal."

What do you call a person like me who hears messages from God and passes them on? Do you think that would be an easy job? Why or why not?

Elijah swallowed hard and passed God's message on to Ahab. But Ahab only laughed. That is, until it stopped raining.

One year went by.

Another year followed.

And there was not one drop of rain.

So, in the third year, Elijah went to see King Ahab again.

"Elijah, you troublemaker!" Ahab roared. "See what you have done! The crops have died. The wells are dry. And it's *all* your fault!"

"No, Your Majesty," said Elijah. "The fault is yours, for you have not obeyed the Lord God."

Ahab thought that the rain stopping was Elijah's fault, but Elijah said it was Ahab's. Do bad things ever happen because people make bad decisions? Can you think of an example? And what is the problem with them blaming someone else?

"The Lord God – ha!" snapped Ahab. "I don't have to listen to what he says. I follow Baal."

"All right, then," answered Elijah. "Why don't we have a contest – to prove once and for all who the true God really is?"

Was I taking a risk when I asked for a contest? Is there any reason I had confidence that God would win the contest? You might like to have a look at 1 Kings, chapter 17, to see what happened before the challenge.

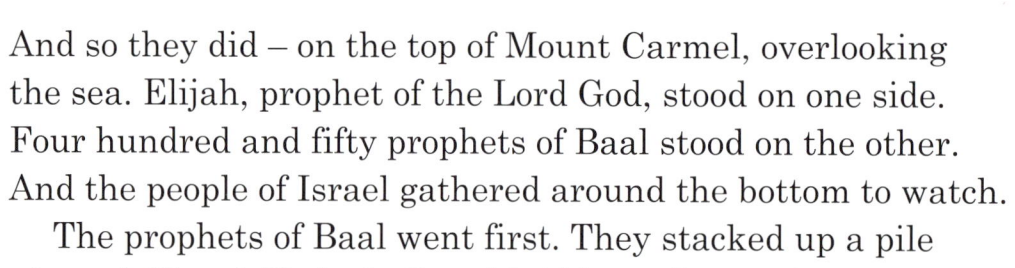

And so they did – on the top of Mount Carmel, overlooking the sea. Elijah, prophet of the Lord God, stood on one side. Four hundred and fifty prophets of Baal stood on the other. And the people of Israel gathered around the bottom to watch.

The prophets of Baal went first. They stacked up a pile of wood. They killed a bull and laid it on the top. Then they prayed to Baal, and asked him to set the whole thing on fire. They prayed hard. They prayed long – from breakfast to lunchtime. But there was no fire. Not even a spark.

Elijah couldn't resist having a little fun. "Perhaps Baal is asleep," he joked. "Or day-dreaming, or on holiday! Or maybe he's just a little hard of hearing."

Why do you think I poked fun at the prophets of Baal?

So Baal's prophets prayed louder. But it made no difference, and by the middle of the afternoon they were exhausted.

And that's when Elijah took his turn. He piled up twelve stones – one for each of the sons of Jacob. He laid wood on top of that, then the bull. Finally he poured water over the whole thing!

The crowd was amazed. How would it ever catch fire? But Elijah knew just what he was doing. "Lord," he prayed, "you are the real God. Please show that to your people now, so they will follow you again."

Elijah had barely opened his eyes when it happened. God sent fire from heaven that burned up not only the bull, but the stones, and wood, and water, as well!

"The Lord is God!" the people shouted.

Then they cheered for Elijah, chased away the prophets of Baal, and ran for cover. Because suddenly it had started to rain!

💡 Why do you think Elijah poured water over the altar? It might help to remember what the weather had been like the previous three years!

📶 Talk about what would be the best thing about being a prophet. What would be the hardest thing?

Are there prophets today? If you think there are, who might they be? What do they do?

💡 Can you think of a time when you had to stand up for what was right? Can you think of someone else who has done that?

📝 List the relationships in this story – the USes. And is there anyone so concerned about ME that it causes trouble?

⏸ Pray for the courage to stand up for what's right, even when the majority of people think the opposite.

Jonah the Groaner

Hi! My name is Jonah. And this is my story. You can also read it in the Bible. It's the whole of the book of Jonah in the Old Testament (and it's not very long).

As you read it through, groan, if you like, whenever Jonah groans.

Jonah was a groaner.

That's right – a groaner.

So when God told him to go to Nineveh and tell the people who lived there to change their evil ways, what did Jonah do?

Jonah groaned.

"Not Nineveh!" he groaned. "Anywhere but Nineveh! The people who live there are our enemies!"

What do you think I'm thinking?

And when he had stopped groaning, Jonah bought himself a ticket. A ticket for a boat ride. A boat ride that would take him far away from Nineveh.

God listened to Jonah groan. God watched him buy his ticket. But God still wanted Jonah to go to Nineveh.

So when the boat reached the deepest part of the sea, God sent a storm.

"God, help us!" cried a sailor. "We're sinking!"

"God, save us!" cried another. "We're tipping over!"

"God must be very angry," cried the captain, "with someone here on board."

And what did Jonah do? Jonah groaned.

"It's me," Jonah groaned. "I'm the one God's angry with. He told me to go to Nineveh, and here I am, sailing in the opposite direction. Throw me into the sea and your troubles will be over."

"God, forgive us!" the sailors cried as they tossed Jonah into the water. And almost at once, the sea grew calm.

"Oh dear," Jonah groaned, "I'm sinking."

"Oh no," Jonah groaned, "I'm going to drown."

"Oh my," Jonah groaned, "that's the biggest fish I've ever seen!"

And before he could groan another groan, the fish opened its mouth and swallowed Jonah up!

What do you think I'm thinking now?

It was God who sent the fish – to rescue Jonah, and to give him time to think. He had plenty to groan about, of course – the fish's slimy stomach, the seaweed, the smell.

But Jonah was still alive – and that was something to cheer about! So Jonah stopped his groaning and said a prayer:

"I was sinking, Lord. I was drowning. But you saved me. So now I will do whatever you want."

Three days later, the fish spat Jonah up on a beach. And Jonah kept his promise – he went straight to Nineveh and told the people that God wanted them to change their evil ways.

"Forty days is all you've got," he warned them. "And if you haven't changed by then, God will destroy your city."

The people of Nineveh listened. The people of Nineveh wept. Then the people of Nineveh changed! From the king right down to the poorest slave, they decided to do what was right.

And what did Jonah do? Jonah groaned. He sat himself down in the shade of a tree and he groaned.

"I knew this would happen," he groaned. "You are a loving God who loves to forgive. But I still

What do you think I'm thinking at this point in the story?

don't like the people of Nineveh and I wish they had been destroyed."

Jonah fell asleep groaning. And during the night, God sent a worm to kill the tree. When Jonah awoke, he groaned more than ever.

"The tree is dead!" he groaned. "And now I have no shade."

"Oh, Jonah!" God sighed. "You pity this tree. Yet you did not plant it or water it or grow it. Do I not have the right to pity the people of Nineveh – 120,000 and more, and all their cattle? More than 120,000 who do not know wrong from right."

And what did I do? Did I groan? Did I agree? Did I tell God I was sorry? No one knows, because the story does not tell us. Perhaps that's because the story is really about the hearts of those who hear it. And the answer lies in how you would have responded if you were me!

Where did this story happen? What different places did I visit? Now think about how each place is important to my story.

What do you think is the main problem in Jonah's story? (Hint: it's not just that he disobeyed God.) Are there any other problems? What was God doing in Jonah's story? Did God help solve the problem?

Have you ever felt like Jonah felt in the story? Did you ever face a problem like he faced? Where was God in that?

Make a list of the different characters and how Jonah related to them. Is there anyone so concerned about ME that it causes trouble?

Why not pray about anything that has troubled you, or challenged you, or helped you in this story?

Daniel and the Lions

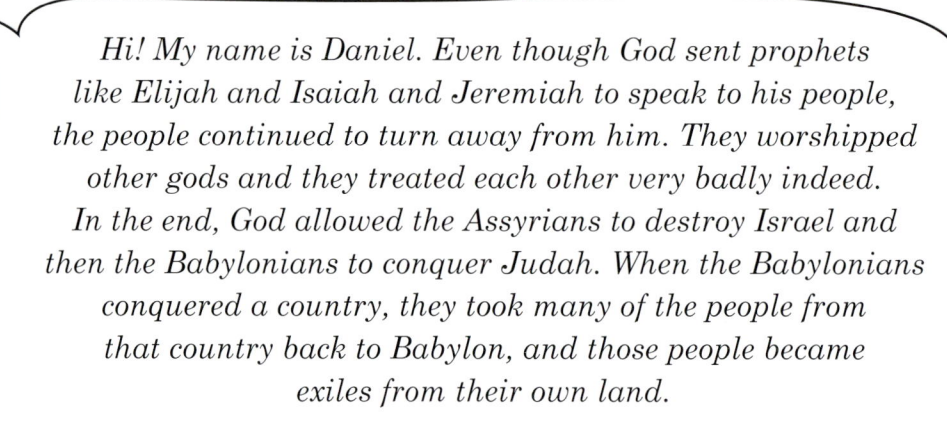

Hi! My name is Daniel. Even though God sent prophets like Elijah and Isaiah and Jeremiah to speak to his people, the people continued to turn away from him. They worshipped other gods and they treated each other very badly indeed. In the end, God allowed the Assyrians to destroy Israel and then the Babylonians to conquer Judah. When the Babylonians conquered a country, they took many of the people from that country back to Babylon, and those people became exiles from their own land.

The Babylonians also chose the brightest and best young people from that conquered land, treated them well, sent them to their schools, and tried to make good Babylonians out of them – in hopes that such treatment would help all the exiled people settle in their new home. That's what happened to me and my friends.

It was hard to adapt to a new way of life in a foreign country and still be faithful to God. But with God's help, that's what I managed to do. I became a trusted adviser to the king of Babylon. And even when Babylon itself was conquered by the Medes and Persians, I was able to help that new king as well. But that made the king's other advisers jealous of me…

During this story, roar with the lions. Lick your lips with the lions. Skulk away, whimpering with the lions.

What do you think it was like to be taken as a captive to a foreign land? How was I treated? And why do you think I worked so hard?

Daniel missed his home in Jerusalem. But he wanted to please God, wherever he was, so he worked hard at the jobs he was given – so hard that he became one of the king's own helpers!

But he never forgot about God, or failed to pray to him, morning, noon, and night.

Why do you think I refused to forget about God and continued to pray to him?

Some of the king's men were jealous of Daniel. They wanted his job for themselves. So they talked the king into making a new law – a law that said, "No one, but no one, is allowed to pray to anyone but the king himself."

"We've got Daniel now!" his enemies laughed.

And so they had. For the very next morning, Daniel knelt by his window, bowed his head, and prayed – not to the king, but to God.

"Thank you for taking care of us in this faraway land," he prayed. "Forgive us, and please take us back to our own land soon."

Daniel's enemies were watching. And before he could even open his eyes, they grabbed him and dragged him in front of the king.

Why do you think the king's men were jealous of Daniel? Has anyone ever been jealous of you? Why?

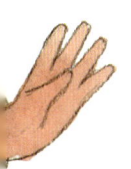

The king was sad. Very sad. He liked Daniel. But he could not break his own law.

"Daniel must be punished," he sighed. "Throw him into the lion pit."

Why do you think I was sad when I had to punish Daniel?

But even as the king gave the order, he whispered a prayer that no one could hear. A prayer to Daniel's God that, somehow, Daniel might be saved.

The pit was dark. The pit was deep. The lions covered its floor like a shaggy growling carpet. They leaped to their feet in a second when Daniel landed among them. They licked their lips. They showed their teeth. Their eyes shone bright and fierce. They opened their mouths and moved toward their dinner.

And then they stopped.

"Shoo! Scat! Go away!" shouted a voice right behind Daniel.

How do you think you might have felt if you were dropped into a pit filled with lions like us?

The lions' mouths snapped shut. Their tails drooped. And they whimpered away to the corners of the cave.

Slowly Daniel turned around, and looked up into the face of an angel!

"Nothing to worry about now," the angel smiled. "God sent me to watch over you. Why don't you get some sleep?"

Why do you think I was able to go to sleep in a lions' den?

The next morning, the king cheered when he discovered that Daniel was still alive.

"Pull Daniel out," he ordered his men. "And while you're at it, take the men that talked me into that silly law and dump them into the pit instead."

The king put his arm around Daniel and walked him back to the palace.

Meanwhile Daniel's enemies cried for help. And the lions enjoyed their breakfast!

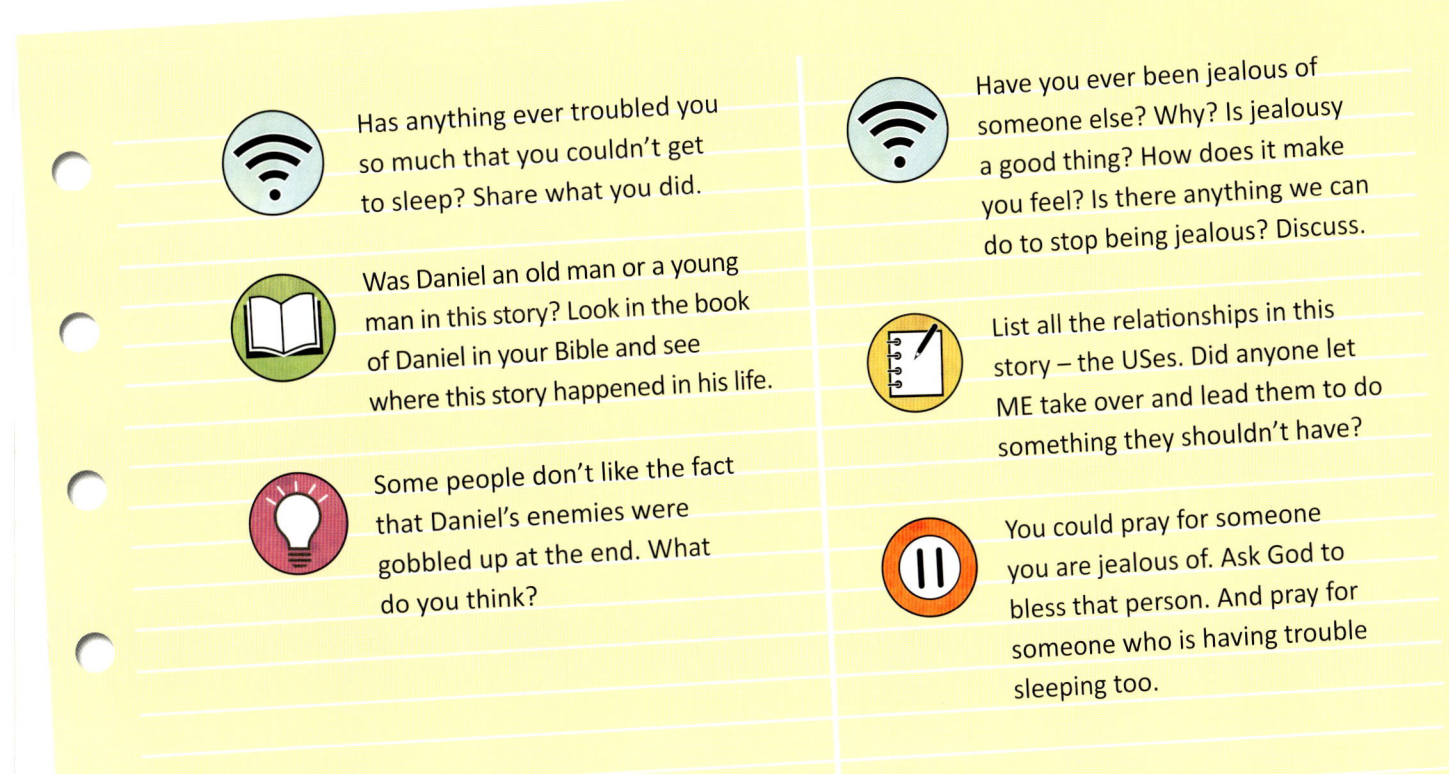

Has anything ever troubled you so much that you couldn't get to sleep? Share what you did.

Was Daniel an old man or a young man in this story? Look in the book of Daniel in your Bible and see where this story happened in his life.

Some people don't like the fact that Daniel's enemies were gobbled up at the end. What do you think?

Have you ever been jealous of someone else? Why? Is jealousy a good thing? How does it make you feel? Is there anything we can do to stop being jealous? Discuss.

List all the relationships in this story – the USes. Did anyone let ME take over and lead them to do something they shouldn't have?

You could pray for someone you are jealous of. Ask God to bless that person. And pray for someone who is having trouble sleeping too.

A Surprise for Mary

Hi! My name is Mary. Four hundred years or so after God's people returned from exile, God finally made good on the promised saviour he always said he would send – Someone Special who would rescue everyone from the wrong things they had done. Amazingly, that story began with my cousin Elizabeth and me!

You might want to scream with Mary, tremble with Mary, sit there with your mouth open with Mary, and nod quietly with Mary as she moves from one emotion to another during her encounter with the angel.

Gabriel was a busy angel! He visited an old man called Zechariah and told him that his equally old wife, Elizabeth, would have a baby! Then he went to work again.

What do you think that Zechariah thought when I told him that he and his wife would have a baby? (You can read about it in the first chapter of the Gospel of Luke). Does this story remind you of any story in the Old Testament? Which one? How did those people react to the news?

Six months after Elizabeth discovered that she would have a child, Gabriel visited Elizabeth's cousin Mary.

Mary and Elizabeth were quite different.

Elizabeth lived in the south, near the big city of Jerusalem. But Mary lived way up north, in a village called Nazareth.

Elizabeth was old.
But Mary was young.

And Elizabeth had been married for many years, but Mary had never been married at all. She was engaged, however, to a carpenter named Joseph.

Mary was in her house one day, dreaming of the wedding and the life that she and Joseph would share together. And that's when Gabriel appeared to her – bright and shiny, glowing and gold – just as he'd appeared to old Zechariah.

"Hello, Mary," Gabriel said. "God is with you and wants to do something very special for you."

Mary didn't know what to think. She had never seen an angel before. And as for God wanting to do something special for her – well, she couldn't imagine what that might be. She was too scared to ask, and Gabriel could see the worry in her eyes.

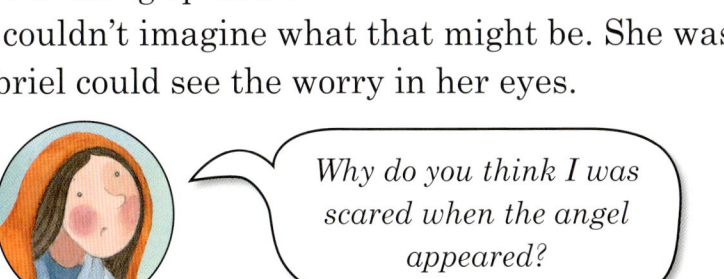

Why do you think I was scared when the angel appeared?

81

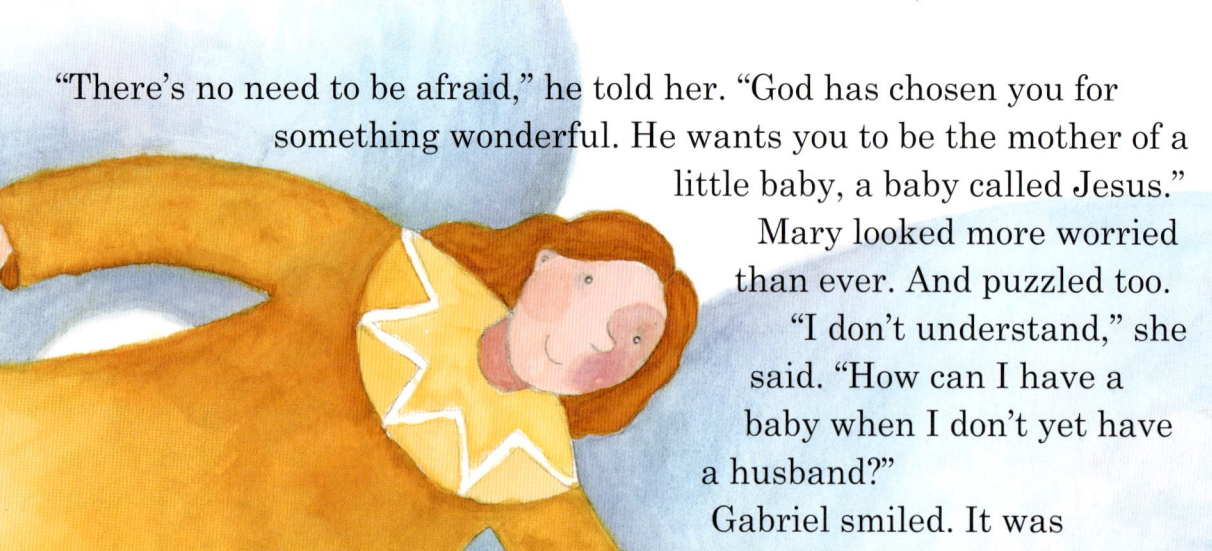

"There's no need to be afraid," he told her. "God has chosen you for something wonderful. He wants you to be the mother of a little baby, a baby called Jesus."

Mary looked more worried than ever. And puzzled too.

"I don't understand," she said. "How can I have a baby when I don't yet have a husband?"

Gabriel smiled. It was a warm smile. And a mysterious smile too.

"God's own Spirit will visit you," he said. "Like a welcome shadow on a warm summer's day, he will cover you and wrap himself around you. And the child who will spring to life in you will be God's child too."

Mary was shaking now. Her eyes were wide open, amazed. Her mouth dropped open too. She had never heard anything like this before!

"I know this is hard to believe," Gabriel went on. "But God can do the most amazing things. Why, your own cousin Elizabeth – that's right, Elizabeth, who could never have a child before – is expecting a baby too! Impossible? Not for God! So what do you say, Mary? Will you be the mother of God's Son?"

So much of what the angel told me was amazing. What do you think was the most amazing thing about his message?

82

Mary shut her eyes. She shut her mouth too.

She looked just as if she was praying.

What will Joseph think, she wondered, when he hears about the child? He is bound to think the worst. And my parents too. Their plans, all their plans, will be ruined! And yet, God has a plan as well. And he has chosen me – me of all people – to be a part of that plan. What can I do but say yes?

And so Mary nodded. Eyes still shut, head bowed in prayer, she nodded.

"I will do it," she said. "I will be the mother of God's Son."

And when she opened her eyes, the angel was gone.

Discuss why you think Mary agreed to be the mother of God's Son, even though it was likely to make her life more difficult. Can you name any other people in the Bible who agreed to do something God asked, even though it made their life harder? Do you know anyone, in your church maybe or your family, who has done something God asked that then made their life more difficult?

Another name for Jesus is Emmanuel, which means "God with us". Why do you think God decided to come and live among us? How does it make you feel to think that God was growing in Mary's womb, was born like any other baby, and was a toddler and child?

Who were the people in this story who put US before ME?

One, two, three.

Four, five, six.

Seven, eight, and nine.

Mary counted the miles. And the number of times the little baby kicked inside her belly.

It was a long trip. And a hot trip. And she prayed that it would soon be over.

One, two, three.

Four, five, six.

Seven, eight, and nine.

Mary knew, because she counted, that there were many more miles to go.

When they arrived, at last, in Bethlehem, Mary and Joseph looked for a place to stay.

One, two, three.

Four, five, six.

Seven, eight, and nine.

And there, at house number ten, was the home of one of Joseph's relatives. It was his home town after all, remember.

The door opened. Joseph's relative smiled. But when Joseph asked if he had an empty room, the relative sadly shook his head.

"The house is bursting," he said with a sigh. "The upstairs rooms are filled with your aunties and uncles and cousins."

"But Mary…" Joseph said. "Mary, my wife, is expecting a baby."

"I can see that," the relative nodded, glancing at her belly. And then he stopped. And then he thought. And then he said, "But the downstairs room, where we keep the animals, has a bit of space. It's nothing fancy, mind you. But it's warm and dry. You can stay there, if you don't mind."

So that's where they stayed. And when her time came, Mary gave birth there, among the animals, to God's own special Son.

But what about the innkeeper? You may have seen him in a Nativity play. Well, the fact is that the Bible never says there was an innkeeper. The word that is often translated "inn" is exactly the same word Luke uses at the end of his Gospel for the upstairs room where Jesus and his disciples ate a meal together. That's where guests stayed in the houses in those days. And that's what was full up, not a hotel, when Mary and Joseph arrived in Bethlehem. The house probably belonged to one of Joseph's relatives. (Bethlehem was where his family was from.) So Mary and Joseph might have stayed in the downstairs room, which also housed the animals during the night.

If you were on a long journey and needed help, which of your relatives would you turn to? What's the best thing about staying with relatives?

What do you think would be the hardest thing about staying in a room that was also home to animals?

What does it say about God that his Son was born in a place where animals were kept?

What are the USes in this story – the relationships? Does ME get in the way anywhere?

87

The Wise Men's Visit

Hi! I'm one of the star-watchers. People think there were three of us. You may even know a song about that! It's only because there were three gifts mentioned – have a look at Matthew, chapter 2. We did look for signs in the sky, though. And when we saw one, we investigated. And that's how this story begins.

Zig and zag with the star-watchers on their journey.

The sky was black. The night was clear. The stars were bright as diamonds.

"Perfect," said a star-watcher. "Just as it should be." But just then God nudged the brightest star and sent it floating like a kite across the night sky.

"Quick," called the star-watcher to his friends. "Come and see. There's a new star and that means…"

"… a new king!" said another star-watcher. "A new king of the Jews!"

"I'll tell you what," said one more star-watcher, "let's follow the star and see if we can find him."

Why do you think God sent this starry announcement to us, people who lived far away in a different country?

So the star-watchers climbed onto their camels and set off after the star. When it zigged, they zigged. When it zagged, they zagged – across deserts and mountains and rivers. Until they reached the land of God's people, the Jews.

"We have come a long way," explained one star-watcher to King Herod.

"We have followed a remarkable star," explained another star-watcher.

"So can you tell us where the baby is?" asked one more star-watcher. "The baby born king of the Jews?"

"King of the Jews? King of the Jews?" King Herod repeated, trying hard not to look upset. "Let me speak with my advisers."

And so King Herod called a meeting. A meeting that was not very happy.

"King of the Jews?" the king shouted. "King of the Jews? I AM THE KING OF THE JEWS!!"

Why do you think I was upset when I heard that there was a new baby king of the Jews?

"Y-yes, Your Majesty," his advisers mumbled. "But God has always promised that one day he would send us a special king. P-perhaps he is the one the star-watchers are looking for."

"Hmm," Herod muttered. "And where does God say this special king will be born?"

"In B-Bethlehem, Your M-Majesty. The city of D-David," the advisers stammered.

> What do the advisers call the special king whom God promised to send to his people? See Matthew 2.

"Send for the star-watchers," King Herod ordered. "I have decided what I shall do."

"Gentlemen," said the king, "the child you seek is somewhere in Bethlehem. Go to him. Find him. Then come and tell me where he is, so that I can visit him too."

The king said this with a smile, but his heart was black, black as a night without stars. For he had already determined to kill the child, so no one would take his place as king.

Stop looking at me that way! This baby wasn't the first person I decided to kill so I could hang on to my throne. You might want to research my life and see how many others there were!

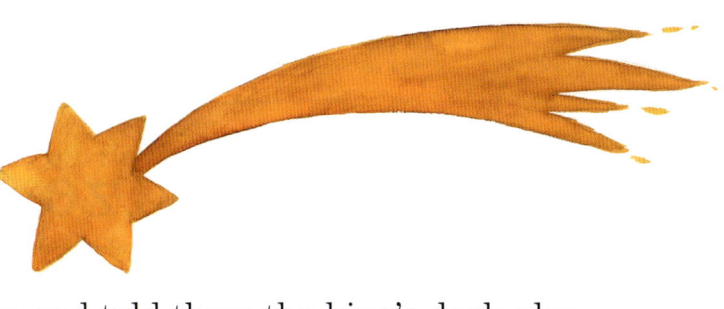

The star-watchers didn't know that when they left, but they soon found out. For the same God who had nudged the star visited them in a dream and told them the king's dark plan. So they went to see young Jesus, and gave him gifts of gold and frankincense and myrrh. And then they went straight home, with stars in their eyes and God in their hearts.

Why did the star-watchers give little Jesus gold, frankincense, and myrrh? Why didn't they give a toy camel, or something else a child could play with?

Has anyone ever tried to take away something that was important to you? How did you react? Does that help you to understand how Herod might have felt? This is not to excuse what he did, not at all, but sometimes people do awful things when they think they will lose something. Can you think of any other examples from history or the news? Discuss.

Why do you think the star-watchers were willing to travel such a long way to see the new king?

What are the relationships in this story – the USes? And where does ME threaten to make a mess of things?

You could pray that people all around the world will have the chance to meet Jesus, like the star-watchers did. You might want to pray for guidance as to how you might help them.

"And what about us?" shouted some Very Religious People.

"You," John shouted, louder than ever, "You snakes! You need to stop pretending that you're perfect – and admit that you have done things that make God sad! I'll say it again – God is sending Someone Special! And you – all of you – need to get ready to meet him. So come, let me dip you in this river to show God that you want your lives to change."

> The religious leaders thought they were pretty good and that they didn't need to repent to get ready for God's kingdom. Why do you think John called them snakes? Why do you think they needed to repent?

The people came. John dipped them in the river. And then, one day, when all the shouting and dipping was done, someone else came too.

It was Jesus. Thirty years old now and all grown up. John recognized him right away, and stopped his shouting. "You're the Special One, aren't you?" he whispered. And Jesus just smiled.

"That's right," Jesus said. "And I want you to dip me too."

"Oh, no," John said. "It should be the other way around!"

"Listen," said Jesus. "It's time I began the work I was sent to do. And this is how my Father wants me to get started. It's the right thing to do."

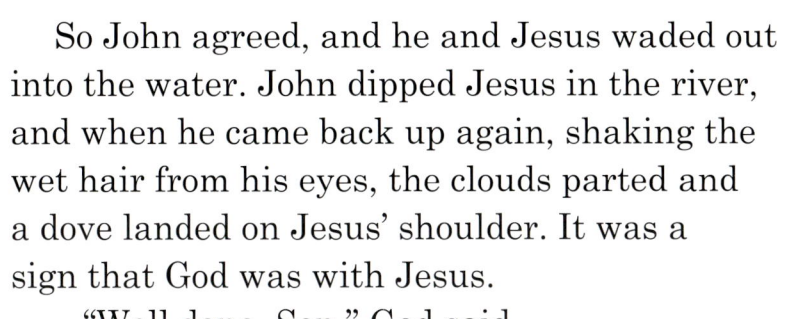

So John agreed, and he and Jesus waded out into the water. John dipped Jesus in the river, and when he came back up again, shaking the wet hair from his eyes, the clouds parted and a dove landed on Jesus' shoulder. It was a sign that God was with Jesus.

"Well done, Son," God said.

"I'm proud of you. You really are Someone Very Special."

"Baptism" is the special word we use to describe what happens when Christians get dipped in water. Are there other ways to be baptized? What does it mean? What does it do?

Why do you think Jesus wanted to be baptized?

Have you every repented about anything? How? Why? Talk about it.

List the relationships in this story. How were they (the USes) important to the story? Did ME show up anywhere?

Jesus taught his disciples to pray. As a part of that, he told them to pray for God's kingdom to come. So you could pray that God's kingdom will come in your community or school or workplace. And then talk about what that might mean specifically.

Jesus' Special Friends

Hi! My name is Peter. I was one of Jesus' disciples. We lived with him, and travelled around the country with him, and learned from him. This story is the beginning of that amazing three-year journey. You can find it in Luke, chapter 5. But because there are four Gospels – that is, four books about the life of Jesus, told from four different angles – you can also find different versions of it in Matthew 4, Mark 1, and John 1. The Luke version is the most exciting, though!

Throw out your nets with Peter, then struggle to pull the nets filled with fish back in.

Jesus grew up in a place called Galilee, where there was a large and beautiful lake. And it was there that he began the work God gave him to do.

"God is like a king," he told the people. "And he wants all of you to be a part of his kingdom – to love him and to love each other."

What do you think it means to be a part of God's kingdom? You might like to read some of Matthew – chapters 5, 6, or 7 – to discover some of the things I said about God's kingdom.

People liked to hear Jesus talk. In fact, one morning, the crowd was so huge that Jesus was nearly pushed into the sea.

> Why do you think the people liked to listen to Jesus talk? What is one thing that Jesus said that you like?

"Excuse me," Jesus asked a fisherman, "could I borrow your boat for a while?"

The fisherman's name was Peter. "Of course," he said. "It's doing me no good. I was out all night and didn't catch a thing."

Jesus climbed into the boat. Peter rowed it a little way from shore. And from there, Jesus talked to the crowd. When he had finished, Jesus sent the people home. And then he turned to Peter.

"Let's go a little further out," he whispered. "I'd like to catch some fish."

Peter tossed back his head and laughed. "I told you. My men and I were out all night. We caught nothing!"

Why do you think I might have thought it was strange when Jesus asked me to take the boat out and catch some fish?

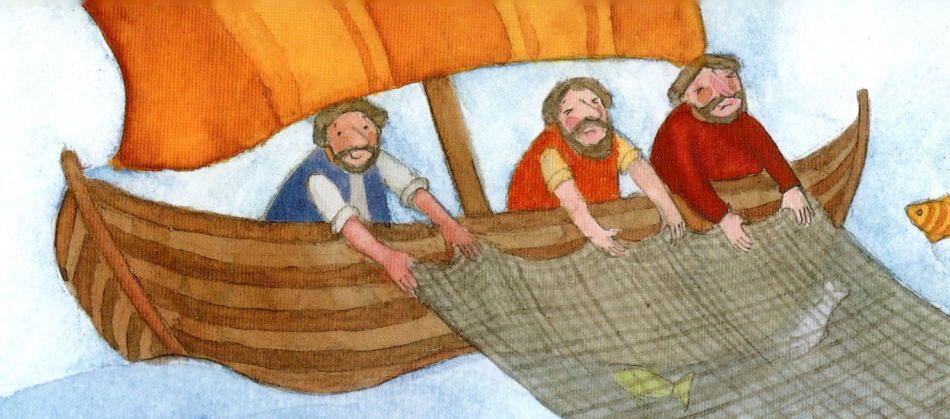

Jesus didn't say a word. He just smiled and looked across the lake.

"All right," Peter sighed. "If that's what you want."

So Peter sailed to the deepest part of the lake. Then he dropped his fishing nets over the side.

It took no time at all. The nets started pulling and jerking and stretching. And it was all Peter could do to keep the boat from tipping over.

"Help!" Peter called to James and John, Peter's partners who were fishing nearby. "Help me, please!" And they rowed to him as fast as they could.

Then, all together, the men pulled on the nets – and the fish came tumbling and slapping onto the decks of both boats. Red fish and blue fish. And not just one or two fish. So many, in fact, that the boats would have sunk had the fishermen not rowed quickly back to shore.

Peter looked at the fish. Peter looked at his friends. Then Peter looked at Jesus, and fell to his knees, trembling.

"Only God, or somebody full of his power, could do that," Peter said. "And why would someone like that want to go fishing with the likes of me?"

Jesus shook his head and smiled. "Don't be scared," he said. "God has given me a lot of work to do. And I need helpers. "Helpers like you and your friends. Once you were fishermen. But from now on, you'll be fishing for people. And helping me bring

> How do you think Peter felt when his nets filled up with fish?

> *Why did I think that somebody like Jesus might not want to be around someone like me?*

100

them to God."
Then Jesus stepped out of the boat and walked away, across the shore.

"Come with me," he called.

Peter and his friends watched him go. They looked at the fish.

They looked at each other. Then they dropped their nets, left their boats behind, and raced off to follow Jesus.

> *It seems like we had a pretty good fishing business. Why do you think we dropped it all to go and follow Jesus?*

What does it mean to go "fishing for people"? What was Jesus asking Peter, James, and John to do? Have you ever gone fishing for people? How?

Why do you think Jesus needed helpers like Peter, James, and John? Why didn't he do the things he did on his own?

Peter, James, and John became Jesus' "disciples". What do you think that means? Can we be disciples of Jesus today? Does it mean the same for us as it did for them?

List the relationships in the story – the USes. Are any new relationships made? How does that happen? How does US in this story make a difference to ME?

You could pray for help as you follow Jesus. Pray for others who follow Jesus too. Pray for help "fishing for people".

"I Can See!"

▶ "I have a question," said one of Jesus' friends. "There's a man here who's been blind since he was born. Did that happen because his parents did something bad?"

"No," said Jesus. "God doesn't punish people by making their children blind. But I'll tell you what – God can use this man's blindness to show us how powerful he is."

> Do you think that God does bad things to us because we have done bad things? Why or why not? But do bad things sometimes happen to us because we have made bad choices? Why is that, do you think?

And with that, Jesus walked over to the man. He knelt down. He spat on the ground. He made a little mud out of the dirt and spit. And he rubbed it on the blind man's eyes. It was very messy!

How do you think I felt when the gooey wet mud unexpectedly touched my eyes?

"Now go and wash your face," Jesus said to the man. "And you will be blind no more."

The man washed his face, just as Jesus said. And when he shook the water from his hair and opened his eyes – he could see!

> What do you think it would be like to suddenly be able to see if you had never seen anything before in your life? What is the first thing you would do if that happened to you?

"We have a question," said the people who gathered around him, later that day. "Aren't you the blind man who usually goes begging for food?"

Why do you think we wanted to know if he really was the man who had been born blind?

"I am," said the man-who-used-to-be-blind.

"Then how can you see?"

"I met a man named Jesus, who rubbed mud in my eyes!"

The crowd was amazed. They were ready to cheer.

And then someone else spoke up, "Excuse me. I have a question too."

This someone was a religious teacher who didn't much like Jesus. Why? Because Jesus was too popular and didn't always agree with what the other teachers said.

"Jesus healed you? And he did it today?" the teacher asked.

"That's right," said the man.

"Well, today is the day of rest – the special day God himself set aside. The day on which no one is allowed to work. But healing is work, surely! So how can this Jesus be on God's side if he breaks God's law?"

Why do you think I was so concerned about Jesus healing the man on the Sabbath, the day of rest? Do you think I had good reasons for objecting to that?

"I don't know," said the man. "But I can see!"

"Because a bad man made you well!" accused the teacher.

"Wait," asked someone else. "How could a bad man do a good thing like that?"

"That's what I want to know," said another. And they asked the man-who-used-to-be-blind all kinds of questions.

"Were you really blind?"

"Were you pretending?"

"Who is this Jesus, anyway?"

It was too much for the man-who-used-to-be-blind. "Listen," he shouted, "I don't know the answers to all your questions, but I do know this. Once I

The man who was no longer blind didn't have any fancy answers for the people. He just told them what Jesus did for him. When you tell someone else what Jesus did for you, that is called a testimony. Can you share something that Jesus has done for you?

was blind, and now I can see. Who but someone sent by God could do a thing like that?"

A little later, as the man was sitting by himself, Jesus came to see him.

"I know it's been a hard day," said Jesus, "but I have a question too. Do you believe that God sent me?"

"I do," said the man. "I really do!"

Jesus smiled. "Then no more questions."

Can you remember a time when a rule got in the way of doing something good for somebody?

Why do you think there were so many questions about the miraculous thing that had happened to this man? Why might it be a good thing to ask lots of questions when someone says they experienced a miracle? Why might it be an unhelpful thing?

Why do you think Jesus performed miracles? John, the author of the Gospel from which this story comes, called Jesus' miracles "signs". Why do you think he called them that?

Do you know anyone who has been healed by a miracle? Share it.

List the relationships in this story – the USes. Was anyone selfish? Did ME get in the way? And was there any way that US made a difference to ME?

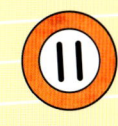

You could pray for someone you know who is ill.

"Time to Get Up"

Hi! My name is Jairus. I was a leader in the synagogue in a town called Capernaum. The synagogue was where Jewish people went to pray and to learn about God. So I would have been very well known in that community. But Jesus not only helped me – a man that everyone knew. He also helped a woman whom no one knew – who was too shy, at first, to even say that she needed his help.

"Jesus! Help me, Jesus! My daughter is dying!" Jairus shouted as loudly as he could, and the crowd parted to let him through.

"She's only twelve," he explained. "And she's so ill. But I know I can count on you to make her well. Please!"

Why did I think that Jesus could make my daughter well? Read Luke 8:41. Do you think my job in the synagogue had anything to do with me trusting Jesus?

Jesus nodded. "Show me the way," he said. But the minute they started wading through the crowd, Jesus stopped.

"Somebody touched me," he announced. "Who was it?"

And when no one in the crowd would admit it, Peter spoke up.

"Jesus," he said, "there are hundreds of people here. I'm sure lots of them touched you!"

"No," said Jesus, raising his voice now. "Somebody here was sick. Very sick. Then they touched me and God made them well. I felt it. I felt the power rush out of me! Now, who was it?"

"It was me," said a woman, trembling. "I have been sick for so long. I've spent so much money on doctors.

> *Why do you think I didn't just walk up to Jesus and ask for his help, like Jairus did? Why did I do it (almost) in secret? And how do you think I felt when Jesus said that someone had touched him?*

But when I touched your robe, I was healed!"

Jesus turned to the woman and smiled. He was so happy for her. "You trusted me," he said. "That's good. So God has made you well."

"Jesus," said Jairus. "Jesus, I don't mean to interrupt…"

> *How do you think I felt when Jesus stopped to deal with the sick woman?*

But before Jairus could say another word, one of his servants called out across the crowd, "Master, master, I have the most awful news…"

Jairus knew it even before the servant spoke.

"… your daughter is dead."

Jesus turned from the happy woman to the sad father. "It will be all right," he said. "Trust me." Then they hurried off to Jairus' house.

What do you think was going through my head when Jesus told me to trust him?

When they arrived, there was another crowd – wailing and weeping in front of the house. The sad news had spread fast.

"Listen, everybody," said Jesus. "There's no need to cry. The girl is not dead. She's only sleeping."

Sad tears gave way to angry laughter. "Don't be ridiculous!" someone shouted. "We've seen her. She's dead!"

Why do you think we laughed when Jesus told us that the girl was just sleeping? Why do you think he said that in the first place?

Jesus ignored them all. He asked the girl's mother and father, and three of his friends, Peter, James, and John, to come with him. Together they walked into the room where the girl was lying.

She certainly looked dead. Her eyes were closed. Her face was pale. Her skin was cold. But that didn't stop Jesus. He took her cold hand in his and called, "Little girl, little girl, it's time to get up."

Her skin grew warm. Her face flushed pink. And her eyelids flickered and flew open. She was alive!

And the first thing she said was, "I'm hungry!"

"Then we'd better get you something to eat," said Jesus.

And it was the best meal that family ever had.

What do you think the little supper was like? What is the first thing you would eat if you had just come back from the dead?

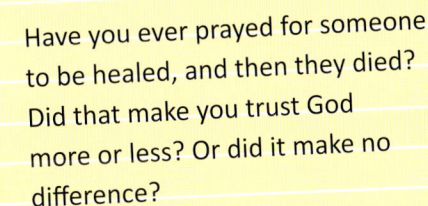

Have you ever prayed for someone to be healed, and then they died? Did that make you trust God more or less? Or did it make no difference?

Jairus lost someone he loved, if only for a short time. Talk about how you felt when you lost someone you loved – a person, or a pet, maybe. What has Jesus done to make it possible for you to see that person again?

What are the relationships in this story? The USes. How do they make things better?

Pray for God's comfort on someone you know who has lost someone they loved.

The Marvellous Picnic

It wasn't long before lots of people wanted to hear Jesus talk about God. And many more wanted him to make them well. So they followed him everywhere. From town to town. From city to countryside. And all the way back again.

What do you think it would be like if people followed you everywhere? Are there people living today who have that problem? Can you name someone?

"We need a rest," Jesus said to his friends one day. So they took a little boat trip across Lake Galilee, hoping to camp for a while in the hills beyond. But the people were so eager to see Jesus that they raced around the shoreline to meet him on the other side!

Jesus was tired. But when he turned and saw the people following him up the hill, he stopped. "They're like sheep without a shepherd," he said to his friends. "They need someone to show them the way."

How are people like sheep without a shepherd? Is that true today? Why or why not?

So he sat himself down – right then and there. And he started to teach.

"God loves you," Jesus said. "He knows what's best for you. The most amazing things can happen when you trust him."

I taught people that God loves them. I taught them that they should trust him. Can you think of anything I did or any stories that I told that showed that? Can you say something else that I taught people? (Hint – you might like to look at Matthew, chapters 5 to 7.)

Jesus said a lot more than that. He taught all day, in fact. And by then, the people were hungry.

"Philip!" Jesus called to one of his friends. "Can you go out and buy some food for these people?"

Philip just laughed. "There are more than five thousand of them! It would take six months' pay to feed them all."

Then Andrew, Peter's brother, spoke up. "There's a boy here, Jesus, who has a little food. Five loaves of bread and a couple of fish. It's not much, but it's a start."

"So it is," grinned Jesus, and he rubbed his hands together, as if he were about to go to work. "Make the people sit down in little groups. Tell them we're going to have a picnic!"

Jesus' friends looked at Jesus. They looked at the boy's little lunch. They looked at the enormous crowd. Then they looked at each other and shrugged.

"All right," they agreed. "Whatever you say."

Jesus smiled as he watched them go. Then he bowed his head, thanked God for the food, and started breaking it into pieces. The friends returned and began to pass out the pieces. And, to their amazement, there was plenty for the first group, and the second group, and the third group, and then every group! Plenty for everyone. More than enough to go around. So much, in fact, that there were twelve baskets full of leftovers to take home!

How do you think you might have felt if you had been the little boy – at the start, when I gave Andrew my lunch? And at the end, after Jesus had fed everyone with it?

The people patted their tummies. They struggled to their feet. They wiped the crumbs from their mouths. And some even burped!

But all Jesus' friends could do was stare.

"It's just as I told you," said Jesus. "God can do the most amazing things. All we have to do is trust him."

Then he smiled at his helpers, popped a chunk of bread into his mouth, and started off for home.

What does this miracle show us about God's love?

What does it show us about his trustworthiness?

Feeding all those people seemed impossible to Philip. Can you give an example of any other place in the Bible where God asks someone to do something that seems impossible?

Jesus feeds hungry people. Did he set an example for us when he did that? How can we feed hungry people? Does that sometimes seem impossible?

What are the relationships in this story? Who put US over ME? And how did that make a difference here?

You could pray for help in trusting God when he asks you to do something hard.

Jesus and the Children

"I can't see!" called a blind woman. "Can you help me, Jesus?"

"I can't walk!" called a lame man. "Heal me, Jesus, please!"

"He can't hear!" called a deaf man's friend. "Touch him, Jesus, and make him well."

They were everywhere – people with every kind of illness. And Jesus felt sorry for them all. So he did what he could to help the crowd that day.

I was really busy that day. Helping and healing people. How do you feel when you get too busy?

"I can't see," said a little girl to her mother. "There are too many people in the way."

"I can't move," said her little brother. "We're all squashed together in this queue."

"What did you say?" asked their father. "I can't hear. This crowd is so noisy!"

"Excuse me," said their mother to one of Jesus' friends. "We were wondering if Jesus could pray for our children."

"Are they sick?" asked the friend.

"No," the mother answered. "We just wanted Jesus to ask God to watch over them and protect them."

"Well," said another friend impatiently, "Jesus is a very busy man. He has important things to do. Lots of sick people to make well."

"Does this mean we won't see Jesus?" asked the little girl, rubbing the tears from her eyes.

But before her mother could answer, another

What do you think is the worst thing about waiting? What do you do to pass the time? What would you do if there were no phones or games or books? That's what it was like for the children in this story.

Have you ever waited for ages to see someone special? How would you have felt if you had waited for ages and then been told to leave?

voice called out across the crowd. "Wait!" It was the voice of Jesus!

"Bring your children here," Jesus called. He gave his friends an unhappy look.

Jesus picked up the little boy and the little girl and set them on his lap. He gave them each a hug, and then he said, "Listen, my friends, you must never keep the children away from me. They are as important to me as anyone else. And I want to be their friend too. Don't you see? God wants us all to be like these children. To love him like a father. To trust him completely. And to long to be with him."

Then Jesus prayed for the children, hugged them one more time, and sent them beaming back to their parents.

Is there any way that grown-ups might be keeping children away from Jesus today? How? Why does Jesus want his followers to be like children?

Why do you think Jesus went out of his way to make sure that his disciples knew that children were important?

List the relationships in this story – the USes. How do those good relationships make things better?

Are there any places where ME gets in the way?

You could name a young friend that you know and pray that they will get to know Jesus.

Jesus and the Taxman

Hi! My name is Zacchaeus. I was a tax collector who lived in Jericho, not far from Jerusalem. I was curious about Jesus. I wanted to see him when he came to my town. But there were problems with that, as you will see! If you want to read the story in the Bible, you can find it in Luke, chapter 19.

As you read the story, you could shout the lines that the people in the crowd shout.

"Jesus is coming!" somebody shouted. "Jesus is coming to Jericho!" And everybody ran to meet him.

Well, almost everybody. For there was one man – one wee little man – who did not run to meet Jesus. And his name was Zacchaeus.

It's not that Zacchaeus didn't want to see Jesus. He did. He really did. But, not only was Zacchaeus short, he was also afraid of the crowd. Not many people liked him, you see. Partly because he was a tax collector. Partly because he collected taxes for the Romans, who had conquered their land. And partly because he collected more taxes than he was supposed to – and kept what was left for himself.

Why do you think we disliked Zacchaeus so much? Was it just because he was a tax collector?

"Jesus is here!" somebody shouted. "Jesus is here in Jericho!" And everybody cheered as he walked through the city gates.

Well, almost everybody. For Zacchaeus did not feel like cheering at all. He wanted to see Jesus. He really did. But how could he walk out there in front of all those people he'd cheated? And what would they do if they got hold of him?

Then Zacchaeus had an idea. There were trees by the city gates – sycamore fig trees. If he could sneak behind the crowd and climb one of those trees, he could see Jesus – and not be seen himself!

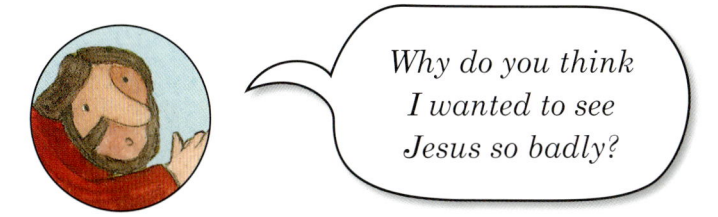

Why do you think I wanted to see Jesus so badly?

So off he went – out of his house and through the empty streets. And because the crowd was watching Jesus, he had no trouble at all slipping behind them and clambering up a tree.

"Come, eat at my house!" somebody shouted. "Come, eat at my house, Jesus!" And because it was a great honour to host someone as important as Jesus, everybody shouted at once.

Well, almost everybody. For there was one man – one wee little man – who kept his mouth shut and tried hard not to rustle the branches.

I would probably have been quite a rich man. What was odd about me climbing a tree?

"Thank you very much," said Jesus. "You are very kind. But I have already decided where I will eat my dinner."

Then Jesus looked straight at the trees and called, "Zacchaeus! Zacchaeus, come down! I'm eating at your house today."

"Zacchaeus?" somebody shouted. "Jesus is eating with Zacchaeus? He's the worst man in town. There must be some mistake!" And everybody moaned and groaned.

Well, almost everybody. One man – one wee little man – climbed down from the tree, as shocked as the rest. Why would someone as good as Jesus want to eat with someone bad like him? But he was happy too. Happier than he'd been for a long, long time. And so, with a smile spreading across his face, Zacchaeus led Jesus to his house.

How do you think you would have felt if you had asked Jesus to your house and he had chosen to go to Zacchaeus' house instead?

Why do you think I chose to go to Zacchaeus' house?

"What are they saying?" somebody whispered. "What are they doing in there?" And everybody gathered around the taxman's door.

118

That's when Zacchaeus threw open his door with a bang!

"Greetings, everyone!" he shouted. "I have an announcement to make. I've been talking with my new friend, Jesus, and realize that there are a few things I need to change. I've cheated some of you. I admit that. And I want you to know that I'm sorry. So sorry, in fact, that I will pay you back four times more than I stole from you! What's more, I intend to give half my money to the poor!"

Why do you think I gave all that money away?

The crowd was shocked. Never, in their whole lives, had they seen anyone change like that! They stood there with their mouths wide open. And nobody said a thing.

Well, almost nobody.

"Don't you see?" said Jesus to the crowd. "God has sent me to share his love with everybody – even those who have done some very bad things. That's what I have done. And now Zacchaeus loves God too."

That's when the crowd began to cheer. Jesus. And Zacchaeus. And the whole town of Jericho. Everybody.

Are there "good" people and "bad" people? What do you think people mean when they say things like that? Does it have to do with who those people are, or with their actions?

Is there anyone you think Jesus should visit for dinner?

Talk about anything else Jesus said or any stories he told that make the same point he made to the crowd after his dinner with Zacchaeus.

List the relationships in this story. How did US make a difference to ME?

You could pray for someone you know who is on the edge of things – who perhaps feels that no one likes them.

119

The Father and His Two Sons

Hi! I'm the father in this story. And yes, I am a made-up character in one of Jesus' stories! Jesus told lots of stories to help people understand the kingdom of God. They are a particular kind of story called parables, because there is a special meaning to discover, hidden within the story itself. Sometimes, as in the case of the story of the sower in Luke, chapter 8, Jesus explained the meaning. Sometimes he didn't, and he left his audience to ponder and to wonder at the meaning. This story is the third of three stories that Jesus told about "lost" things. You can find it in Luke, chapter 15.

The people who thought they were good were not happy with Jesus. They moaned. They grumbled. They frowned.

"It's not fair," they complained. "Jesus spends all his time with the bad people."

So Jesus told them a story…

Why do you think the religious leaders were unhappy about Jesus spending time with people they thought were bad?

Once upon a time there was a man who had two sons. He loved them both, very much. But one day, the younger son came to him with a sad request.

"Father," the younger son said, "when you die, I will get part of your money and part of your land. The problem is, I don't want to wait. I want my money now!"

It was all the father could do to hold back his tears. But because he loved his son, he agreed, and gave him

Why do you think I wanted my father's money right away? Was that a good thing? A bad thing? What was I saying about my father when I asked for it?

his share of the money.

That very day the son left home, money in his pocket, and a big smile on his face. He didn't even say goodbye. The father just watched, wiped away a tear, and hoped that one day he would see his son again.

Was it a good idea to give my son the money? Did I have a choice? What do you think might have happened if I had said no?

The son travelled to a country far, far away and spent his money just as fast as he could. He used his money to do many bad things – until finally the money was gone.

The son looked for a job, but the only work he could find was taking care of pigs! It was hard, dirty work, and he was so hungry sometimes that he thought about taking the pigs' food for himself.

How do you think I spent the money? What's so bad about having a bit of fun? How do you think my father would have felt if he could see me and my friends?

He was miserable, lonely, and sad. And then one day, he had an idea.

"The servants who take care of my father's animals are much happier than I am. I'll go home, that's what I'll do. I'll tell my father how sorry I am for wasting his money. And maybe, just maybe, he'll let me become a servant and work for him."

Why do you think I planned to ask my father to be a servant? Why would I not ask to be treated like his son?

What is particularly awful about a Jewish boy having to care for pigs like us?

Now what do you think the father had been doing all this time? Did he say to himself, "I have my eldest son at home with me. Who cares if my younger son is gone?" Of course not! He loved his son, even though he had gone far away. And every day, he would go out to the roadside and watch, hoping his son would return.

That's exactly where he was when the younger son hobbled home, poor and hungry. The father ran to his son and hugged him tight. And the son dropped right to his knees.

I seem to have had lots of money. Why did I just wait for my son to return home? Why didn't I go after him, or send someone to find him and bring him back?

"Oh, Father," he cried. "I'm so sorry. I have wasted all your money and am no longer good enough to be your son."

"Don't be silly," said the father. "You are my son. You will always be my son. And I am so glad to have you back!"

Then the father lifted his son to his feet and walked him home. He dressed him in beautiful clothes. He put gold rings on his fingers. And he threw him a big welcome-home party.

When the elder son came home from work that night, he heard the party noise.

"What's happening?" he asked. And when a servant told him, he was filled with anger and ran to his father.

Say one word to describe how I felt when my father welcomed me back – not as his servant, but as his son.

"It's not fair!" he shouted. "I've been a good son. I've worked hard for you all these years. But he was bad. He wasted your money. And now you're throwing him a party."

Think of one word to describe how I felt when I saw what my father had done for my brother. Do you think I had good reason for feeling the way I did?

"I love you, my son," the father said. "And you have enjoyed all the good things I have. But your brother was gone, and now he's back. He was lost, and now he's found. That's why I'm having this party, because we're all back together again, and it's time to celebrate!"

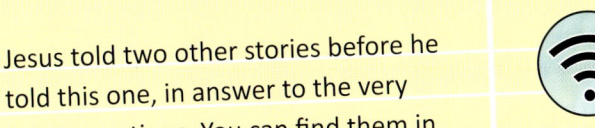

Jesus told two other stories before he told this one, in answer to the very same questions. You can find them in Luke, chapter 15. They are very short. You might like to read them as well, and talk about how they are similar to and different from this story.

Who do you think the younger son is meant to represent? And what about the older son?

Who do you think is meant to represent God in this story? Is God always fair? What might be better than fairness?

Can you share any examples from your own experience of someone who left the people they loved and was then welcomed back? Or perhaps they weren't. What was that like? What was the difference?

List the relationships in this story – the USes. How did ME play a part in the story?

Were there any places where US turned ME into something else?

You could pray for families that have been torn apart. Pray for understanding, for reconciliation, and for healing.

After the robbers had gone, a priest came by, walking down that same road. He saw the man, but instead of stopping to help, the priest just walked past.

Why do you think I might have walked by instead of helping the man?

A little more time passed, and the beaten man was even worse. And that's when a Temple worker came walking by. He saw the man, but instead of stopping to help him, the Temple worker walked past, just like the priest.

More time passed, and by now the beaten man was very unwell indeed. And that's when a Samaritan came walking by.

Why do you think I walked past?

Now the Jews and Samaritans didn't get along. They had been enemies for years and years. But when the Samaritan saw the beaten man, he stopped, he bent down, and he helped the man.

The Samaritan bandaged his wounds. He poured soothing oil on them. He put the man on his donkey. And he took him to an inn so he could rest.

Then the Samaritan gave the innkeeper two silver coins to care for the beaten man, and the promise of more when he returned.

Why do you think I stopped to help the wounded man?

"Now then," Jesus asked the religious teacher. "Which of the men who passed by was a neighbour to the man who had been beaten?"

"It was the one who helped him, the Samaritan," the man answered.

"That's the answer that I would have given," Jesus smiled. "Now go and do the same."

Do we sometimes make excuses for not helping someone? Give an example, if you can. Talk about a time when helping someone else cost you something or was risky.

So who, exactly, is YOUR neighbour?

Why do you think Jesus told the story so that the Jewish man was helped *by* the Samaritan instead of helping a Samaritan? Would it make a difference?

Both Jesus and the religious teacher agreed that we should love God with all that we are and love our neighbours as ourselves. Can you think of a way that those two things overlap?

List the relationships in this story. Who was a good example of US? Who was ME? Does looking at the world and living life from the point of view of US add to *our* list of relationships? How did that work in this story?

You could pray for eyes open enough to see our neighbours' needs, and hearts open enough to help.

The Wise and Foolish Builders

This is another of Jesus' parables. You can find this story in Matthew, chapter 7.

If you want to act it out, someone could be the rock (they can make grunt sounds, fists clenched), and then the sand (they can wave their arms about and go, "Shifty, shifty, shifty"). Someone else could stand as a house (arms over their head like a roof) by the rock and then the sand. Then tell the story and do the appropriate actions when rock, sand, or house is mentioned. Oh and why not act it out outside so someone can be the rain and equip them with a water pistol or super soaker, to drench the rock, sand, and houses at the right time?

Jesus wanted his disciples to know how important it is to follow his example, so he told them a parable that went something like this...

There once was a man.
A wise and clever man.
Who decided to build himself a house.
So he found himself a rock.
A strong and mighty rock.
And on that rock he built himself a house.
And the wind blew.
And the waves rose.
And the rain fell down and down.

But because his house was built

What is a parable? (See page 120.) Why do you think I taught people using parables?

What do you think the house stands for in the parable?

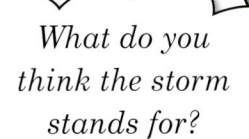

What do you think the storm stands for?

upon a rock,
it did not budge, not one bit.

There once was a man.
A not-so-clever man.
Who decided to build himself a house.
So he found himself some sand.
Some soft and shifting sand.
And on that sand he built himself a house.
And the wind blew.
And the waves rose.
And the rain fell down
and down.

And because his house was built on the sand,
the house fell down with a crash.

"My words," said Jesus, "are like that rock. And if you build your life on them, then you will stand firm too, firm like the house on the rock."

Jesus said that I was a fool. Why do you think he said that?

How do you think my words are like a rock?

This parable appears at the end of Matthew, chapter 7. Why do you think Matthew chose to put it there?

How are lives built on the words of Jesus? What do people need to do to make that happen? Discuss.

Talk about a "stormy" time in your life. How would the words of Jesus have helped? Has there been a time when ignoring Jesus' words or disobeying them made things even stormier for you?

A lot of people think that life is best when we make up our own rules for ourselves and do what we want to do – that no one else has the right to tell us how to live. On the basis of this parable, what do you think Jesus would have to say to that?

Are there any US and ME issues in this story? Are there any places where putting ME first is better or worse than putting US first?

Jesus Rides a Donkey Down the Hill

Hi! We're two of Jesus' disciples. He sent us on a strange mission and then led us on a big parade into Jerusalem, which some people really liked and other people didn't like at all! You can find the story in all four Gospels: Matthew 21, Mark 11, Luke 19, and John 12.

Shout out the hee-haws, hoorays, and moans when they appear in brackets in the story.

"I need a donkey," said Jesus to his friends.
"I need a donkey. (Hee-haw!)
"And if the owner of the donkey should ask you what you're doing,
"Say I need to ride the donkey down the hill.
"I need to ride the donkey down the hill."

When Jesus asked us to fetch him a donkey, it all sounded mysterious: go to this house, untie this donkey, say these words if you are questioned. What do you think was going through our minds as we followed his instructions? How would you have felt?

So Jesus' friends went to find a donkey.
They went to find a donkey. (Hee-haw!)
And when the owner asked, they simply answered,
"Jesus needs to ride the donkey down the hill.
"Jesus needs to ride the donkey down the hill."

Then Jesus' friends put a cloak onto the donkey.
A cloak, not a saddle. (Hee-haw!)
Then Jesus climbed on and headed for Jerusalem.
And Jesus rode the donkey down the hill.
And Jesus rode the donkey down the hill.

The people were surprised when they saw him on the donkey
When they saw him on the donkey. (Hee-haw!)
Then they remembered a promise – a promise from a prophet
About a king who rides a donkey down the hill.

Zechariah was the prophet who foretold that Israel's king would ride on a donkey. You can read the prophecy for yourself in Zechariah 9:9. What is so unusual about a king riding a donkey? What are some of the other things about kings that surprise you in the prophecy?

About a king who rides a donkey down the hill.
So the people cheered when they saw him on the donkey.
The people cheered. (Hooray!)
They cried, "Hosanna! Save us, Lord!"
As Jesus rode the donkey down the hill.
As Jesus rode the donkey down the hill.

Then they laid their cloaks in front of the donkey.
And they laid down palm branches too. (Hooray!)
And they treated Jesus just like a king.
As Jesus rode the donkey down the hill.
As Jesus rode the donkey down the hill.

Why do you think we wanted the people to stop shouting?

Why do you think we cheered and laid down palm branches and cloaks in front of the donkey?

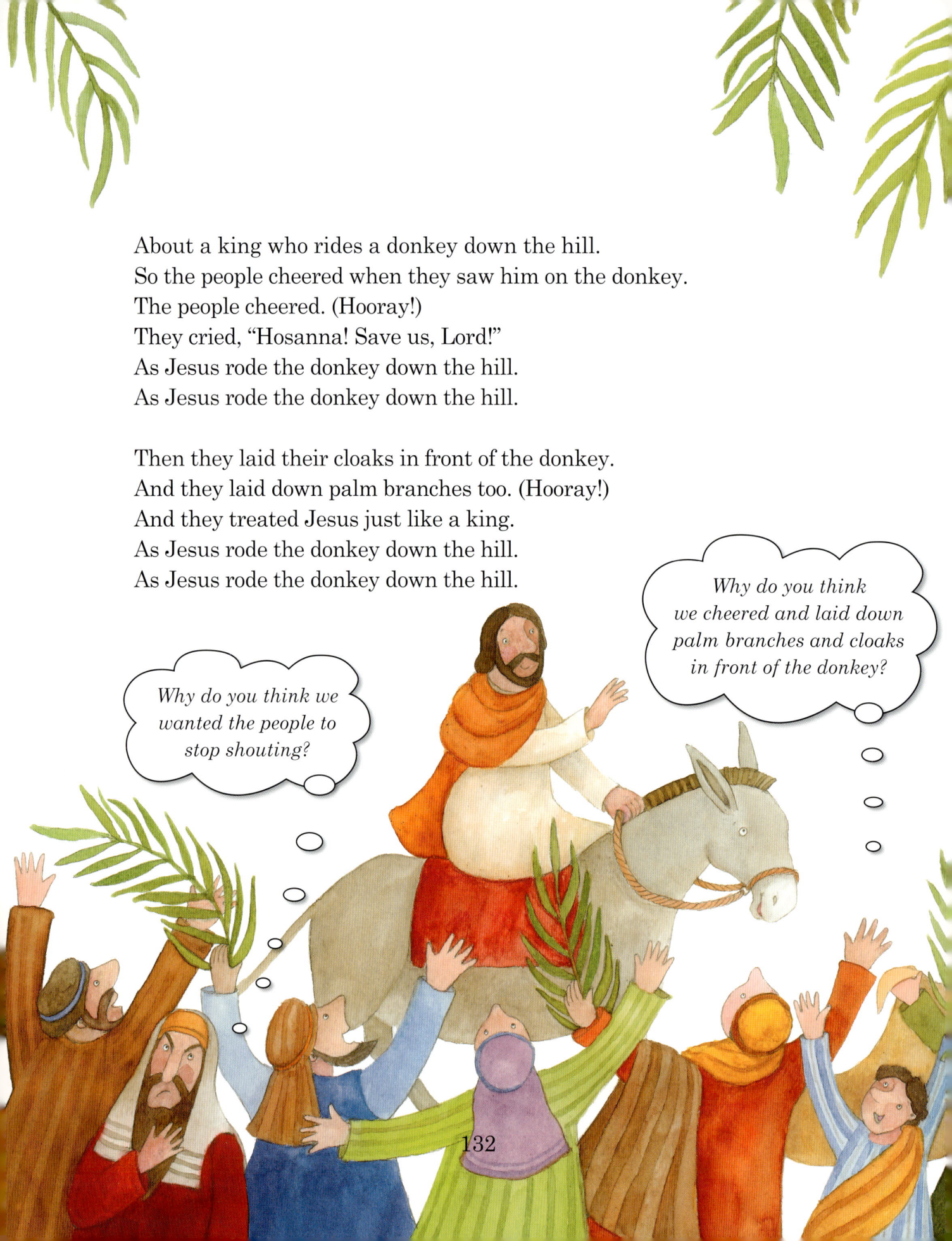

But the religious leaders grumbled and groaned.
They cursed and swore and moaned. (Moan! Moan!)
"You're no king!" they cried. "You're nobody special!"
As Jesus rode the donkey down the hill.
As Jesus rode the donkey down the hill.

"Say what you like!" called Jesus to the leaders.
"Be stubborn as donkeys! (Hee-haw!)
If these stones could speak, they'd join with the people
And cheer the one who rides the donkey down the hill.
And cheer the one who rides the donkey down the hill!"

What do you think Jesus meant when he said that the stones would shout if the people were silenced?

The Roman emperor, Tiberius, was ruler over the land where Jesus lived. How do you think he would have reacted if he had heard that the people in Jerusalem were praising someone else as their king? What kind of a king do you think Jesus meant to be?

What examples of praising God does this story give us? What is your favourite way to praise God?

What are the USes in this story? Was anyone focused just on ME?

You could pray for the courage to speak up for what's true, even if someone else tells you to keep silent.

An Important Meal

Jesus and his twelve friends sat down to eat. There was lamb and bread and wine. A nice meal. But Jesus was sad.

"What's the matter, Jesus?" asked one of his friends.

"I have to go away tomorrow," Jesus sighed. "And I will miss you very much."

Jesus' friends were surprised. "Where are you going?" they asked.

"I am going to be with my Father in heaven," he whispered. "I am going to die."

Why do you think the disciples found it so hard to accept?

Now Jesus' friends were sad too. "There are people here in Jerusalem who do not like me," Jesus explained. "They do not agree with what I teach. They do not believe I come from God. And tomorrow they will arrest me and hurt me and nail me to a cross and kill me."

Make a list of all the reasons that the leaders in Jerusalem wanted to kill me. Then make a list of the reasons that I was willing to die.

"No!" said Jesus' friends. "They will not do that. We will not let them!"

Jesus looked at them sadly. "One of you has already taken money from them and agreed to help them catch me."

Jesus' friends stared at each other.

"Well, it's not me!" said one.

"It's not me," said another.

But one of them – a man named Judas – just looked at Jesus, then stood up and walked out of the room.

"Let him go," Jesus told the others. "We have something more important to do."

And with that, Jesus took a chunk of bread and said a thank-you prayer.

"I will never forget you," he said to his friends. "And I don't want you to forget me either."

Then he broke the bread in half and passed it around. "This is my body," he said. "I give it up for you. Take it and eat it and remember me."

Then he took a cup of wine and said a thank-you prayer for that as well.

"This is my blood," he said. "God will use it to wash away all the bad things anyone has ever done. Take it and drink it and remember me."

Then Jesus and his friends walked out together into the night.

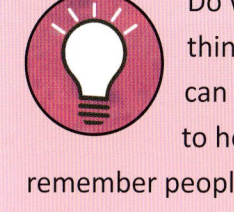

Why do you think I betrayed Jesus?

Do we use things we can touch to help us remember people who are special to us?

Christians believe different things about what happens when we share communion/celebrate the Eucharist. Some Christians believe that it is a way of remembering what Jesus did for us on the cross. Others believe that the bread and wine actually become Jesus' body and blood. If you go to church, what does your church believe? Talk about it.

Jesus' friends said they would be there for him. How did that work out? You might want to read Luke 22:54–62 or Mark 14:43–52.

Who was focused on doing what was best for US in this story? Who was just looking out for ME?

You could pray for anyone you know who has to say goodbye to someone they love.

A Dreadful Day

When Jesus and his friends had finished their goodbye meal, they walked to a garden to pray. That's where Jesus' enemies found him.

The men had torches and clubs and sticks. They were very frightening. And right in front was Judas, who had been one of Jesus' friends.

Judas crept up to Jesus and kissed him on the cheek. "This is the man you want!" said Judas. "Arrest him!"

How do you think I felt when one of my own followers betrayed me to my enemies?

Jesus looked very sad. Jesus' friends were scared. Most of them ran away. But not Peter. He pulled out a sword and started swinging it about.

Why do you think I started swinging my sword about? If you read Luke 22:54–62, you will see what I did later that night. Why do think there was such a change in how I reacted?

"Put your sword away," said Jesus. "This is not the time for fighting. I have to go with them. God wants me to."

So they grabbed Jesus, and dragged him before the religious leaders – the ones who were jealous of him. His trial took all night.

"He says he will destroy our Temple," said one man.

"He says he is a king," said another.

"He's a troublemaker!" said one and all.

None of this was true, of course. But it didn't matter, because the leaders had already made up their minds. Jesus was different from them. Jesus wouldn't do what they said. So Jesus would have to die.

We told lies about Jesus during his trial. Why do you think we did that? Has anyone ever told lies about you? How did that make you feel?

They beat Jesus. They hit him hard. Then they took away his clothes, put an old robe around his shoulders, and jammed a crown made of thorns on his head. And while the blood ran down his forehead, they called him names and made fun of him. "So you think you're a king?" they laughed. "Well, look at you now!"

Jesus never said a word. His body hurt, his heart was breaking, but he never said a word.

Try to imagine, for a moment, what I went through that night. How would you have felt if those things had happened to you? Who do you think I did that for?

They took a cross next, made of heavy wood, and they laid it on his back. "Move along!" they shouted, and they led him through the city. Some people cried when they saw him. Others cheered. But all of them followed, as he lugged that cross through the city gates and up a nearby hill.

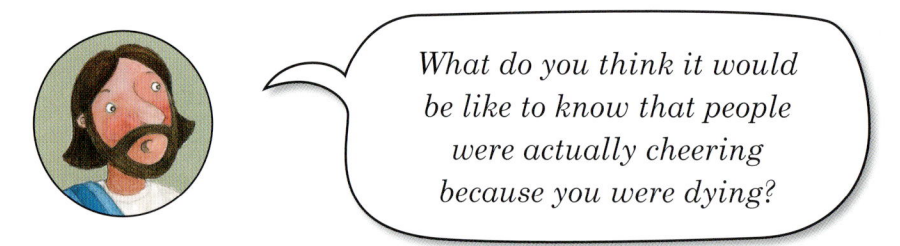

What do you think it would be like to know that people were actually cheering because you were dying?

When they got to the top, they laid Jesus on the cross and nailed him to it. It hurt so much. Then they raised the cross, so that everyone could see, and they left him there to die.

A thief, hanging next to him, was afraid. But Jesus talked to him and helped him feel better.

Jesus' mother was there too, standing in the crowd. So Jesus called to one of his friends, "Take care of her for me, will you, John? She's your mother now."

But most of the faces in the crowd were not so kind. "You saved other people," someone laughed, "so why can't you save yourself?"

Jesus knew why. It wasn't because his enemies had won. It was because God wanted him there – to take away all the bad things anyone had ever done.

Soon the sky grew dark and the earth shook. It was as if God's own heart was breaking. And then it happened.

"It's done," Jesus whispered.

And in the sadness and the dark, he died.

> *Jesus was suffering and dying. Why do you think he took time to talk to me?*

> *Can you say, in your own words, why I died on the cross?*

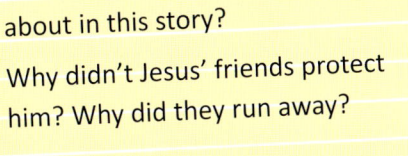

A lot of awful things happen to Jesus in this story. What do you find is the hardest thing to read about in this story?

Why didn't Jesus' friends protect him? Why did they run away?

Through the years, Christians have given lots of reasons for why Jesus had to die. Make a list of all the reasons you think that Jesus died on the cross.

Where is US in this story – the relationships that make things better? And who is only thinking about ME?

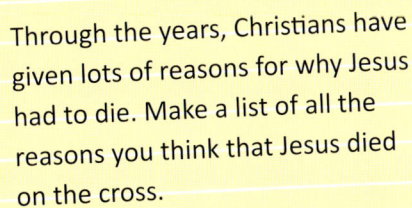

You could pray a thank-you prayer to Jesus for dying on the cross for you.

A Happy Day

It was very early. The birds were still in bed. And the sun had yet to open its bright eye on the world. The sky was grey and grainy. The air was cold. And three women walked slowly toward the graveyard.

Jesus was buried there. And the women were coming to visit his grave.

They talked in sad whispers. They cried. They held each other's hands. Jesus had been dead for three days, and they missed him very much.

Just as they reached the graveyard, however, some surprising things happened. The ground began to shake. The air began to tremble. And, quick as lightning, an angel flashed down from heaven and rolled the stone away from Jesus' tomb!

Everything went quiet. The ground stopped moving. But the women shook with fear.

"Don't be afraid," the angel said. "Come and see. The tomb is empty. Jesus is alive!"

> *How do you think the women might have felt when I announced that their dead friend was now alive? How would you react if an angel told you that someone you loved was alive again?*

Arm in arm, the women crept past the angel and into the tomb. The sheets were still there – the sheets they had wrapped around his dead body. But Jesus himself was gone!

From what we said and did, do you think that we believed the angel?

"Where is he?" asked the women. "What have you done with him?"

"I told you," smiled the angel. "He's not dead any more. He's come back to life. And he wants you to tell all his friends."

The women looked at each other. They didn't know whether to laugh or cry. They could hardly believe it – that is, until they hurried out of the tomb and ran straight into Jesus.

"Oh, Jesus!" they cried. "It's true. You are alive!" And they fell at his feet, amazed!

How do you think the women felt when they saw me? How do you think I felt when I saw them again?

"There's no need to be afraid any more," he said. "God has made everything all right. But I have a job for you. I want you to tell the rest of my friends that I am alive. Tell them I will meet them in Galilee where our adventures all began."

The women waved goodbye and hurried away. The birds were singing now. The sun's bright eye was wide open. And they had the most amazing story to tell.

Jesus didn't just come back from the dead, like Lazarus did (John, chapter 11). He was resurrected. What would you say is the difference? You might find some answers in Luke, chapter 24.

Jesus had actually told his disciples that he would die and be resurrected. Why do you think it was all still a surprise?

What is the first thing you would say to someone you care about if you could meet them again after they died?

How does Jesus' resurrection bring hope to people? You might like to look at 1 Corinthians, chapter 15.

How does this story illustrate the way in which focusing on US can make a difference to ME?

You could say a thank-you prayer to God for Jesus' resurrection. Thank him for the hope it gives us for our resurrection and our reunion with those we love.

Walking and Talking – and Shocking!

Hi! I am Cleopas. This is one of a handful of stories about when Jesus appeared to his followers over the forty days after the resurrection. You might like to read John 20:24–29 to see what happened with Jesus' disciple, Thomas. My story is in Luke, chapter 24.

You might want to join in the story by making a walking and then a talking motion when those two words are mentioned.

Talking and walking. Walking and talking.

The two people travelled from Jerusalem to Emmaus.

It was a three-hour journey, and because the two people were followers of Jesus, there was plenty to talk about. Like the rumour that some of his friends had seen him alive again!

Can you say one thing we might have talked about on our way? Three hours is a long time! Can you say another thing?

So, talking and walking, walking and talking, they made their way.

And then a stranger joined them.

"I hear you talking. I see you walking," said the stranger. "You sound excited. What's it all about?"

"It's about Jesus!" said one of them. A man called Cleopas. "You must be the only visitor to Jerusalem who hasn't heard what happened to him!"

And then, talking and walking, and walking and talking, he explained.

"Jesus was a prophet, sent from God. He did amazing things. Many of us thought he was the messiah – the Special One God promised, to save us from our enemies.

"But the religious leaders sentenced him to death. The Romans killed him on a cross. And all our hopes died with him.

"That was three days ago. But this morning, some of the women who knew him went to visit his tomb. And his body wasn't there! Better still, an angel told them that Jesus wasn't dead any more. That he was alive again!"

What do you think it must have been like for me to listen to Cleopas explain what had happened, when I had just experienced all of it?

The stranger listened carefully. And then, talking and walking, walking and talking, he told the two people what he thought.

"You sound surprised," he said. "Didn't the prophets say that the messiah would have to suffer before he claimed his victory over evil? If this Jesus died, and rose again, then surely that is exactly what happened to him! I think it shows that he is indeed the Special One you've been waiting for."

Then, talking and walking, walking and talking, they came to Emmaus.

"It's late," said the two people to the stranger. "Why don't you stop the night with us?"

And so, talking and walking, walking and talking, they prepared a simple meal.

"Do you mind if I give thanks for the food?" asked the stranger.

"Of course not," both people replied.

So, taking and breaking the bread, he bowed his head and prayed.

And that's when they knew.

The stranger, the man on the road, the one they'd been talking and walking with all afternoon, wasn't a stranger at all.

He was Jesus. Alive again!

How do you think I felt when I realized that our travelling companion was Jesus all along?

But before they could say a thing, Jesus disappeared. He simply wasn't there any more! And they were left alone to wonder.

"We need to tell someone about this!" they cried.
So they hurried back to Jerusalem.
Not talking. Not walking.
But running and jumping for joy!

Why do you think they only recognized Jesus once he broke the bread? You might find a clue in 1 Corinthians 15:35–49.

When Jesus came back from the dead, he appeared many times and in many places. Why do you think he appeared to so many people? In 1 Corinthians 15, the apostle Paul says that over five hundred people saw him!

Talk about why you think that the two people felt the need to make that long journey back to Jerusalem to tell the other disciples what had happened.

Can you think of a time when you were surprised by something Jesus did?

Can you name the USes in this story? Is anyone putting ME first?

We might not literally ever have an experience like the people did on the road to Emmaus. But sometimes people do lovely things for us in the name of Jesus, and surprise us as a result. You could pray for the wisdom to see that when it happens, and for the compassion to "be Jesus", acting like he would, for someone else.

Goodbye at Last

The friends of Jesus were hiding in a locked room, so the men who killed Jesus couldn't find them. Suddenly, Jesus was there with them! They were frightened. They were confused. They thought he was a ghost!

But Jesus said, "Don't be afraid. It's me. Look, here are the marks the nails made in my hands, and the cut the soldier's sword made in my side." Then Jesus joined them for dinner and ate a bit of food – to prove that he wasn't a ghost at all.

Paul said that I had a "resurrected body". On the basis of this story, what do you think a "resurrected body" is like? How does it differ from an ordinary body? How is it different from what we imagine a ghost is like?

A few weeks later, his friends were out fishing. They couldn't catch a thing. Then, all of a sudden, they heard a voice from the shore, calling, "Throw your nets on the other side of the boat!" And when they did, they caught more fish than their boats could hold.

"Wow!" said Peter. "This also happened all those years ago, when Jesus asked us to follow him. It must be him on the beach!" Suddenly, Peter jumped into the sea – clothes and all – and swam back to shore. The other friends followed as fast as they could.

Jesus was cooking fish over a fire. "Sit down by the fire," Jesus said. "Let's have a picnic."

Why do you think Jesus came to us in a similar way to when we first followed him?

After a few weeks, the time came for Jesus to go to heaven and be with God his Father. So he took one last walk with his friends, up a hill where their adventures together had begun.

Read John, chapter 21, to see what happened between Jesus and Peter at the picnic. Why do you think Jesus had that conversation with Peter? There is a clue in John, chapter 18.

"There is something I want you to do," Jesus said, "I will send you a special Helper – God's own Holy Spirit. And with the Holy Spirit's help, I want you to tell my story to the world. Start in Jerusalem, and don't stop until everybody has the chance to follow me. And if you ever feel scared or alone, just talk to me, and I'll be with you."

Why do you think I told my friends to tell my story to the world? Why do you think I told them that I would still be with them?

Then, suddenly, a cloud wrapped itself around Jesus and carried him into the sky. His friends stood and stared, their eyes filled with tears, until two angels appeared.

"Don't be sad," the angels said. "One day, Jesus will come back – in the clouds – just as you've seen him go."

So off the friends went, down the hill – and into the whole world, to tell the story of Jesus.

What does the resurrection of Jesus mean to you? Can you say it in one word?

Why do you think Jesus ascended into heaven? Why didn't he just stay here on earth and travel around telling his own story? Was there any advantage in having his followers do that?

What are the relationships in this story – the USes – that make a positive difference?

You could pray for anyone who wants to tell Jesus' story. Pray for Jesus to help them and be with them as they do. You could write down the name of someone you know who needs to hear Jesus' story.

The Helper Arrives

Jesus told his friends to wait in Jerusalem – to wait for the Helper he'd promised to send them. So they waited. They waited and they prayed for forty days.

And while they waited, the streets of Jerusalem filled up with people from every land. People from the north and from the south. People from the east and from the west. People from all around the world, who came together to celebrate the Feast of Pentecost.

> The disciples had to wait forty days before the Holy Spirit came. Do you think they wondered if anything would ever happen? What might have given them patience? Do you find waiting hard? What's the worst bit?

> Have you ever been anywhere where there were people from lots of different countries, speaking lots of different languages? What was the most interesting thing about that? What was the most difficult?

Jesus' friends were in an upstairs room when suddenly some surprising things began to happen.

They heard a wind blow, harder than the fiercest storm. But nothing was blown about!

They heard the flickering of flames and they watched tongues of fire lick and lap and land on their heads – but nobody smelled any smoke!

And then the Helper came – the Holy Spirit – and he filled them all with the presence and the power of God!

Try to imagine what it must have been like for us when the Holy Spirit came. Think of one word to describe it.

And what they heard next was talking – strange words pouring out of each and every mouth.

So they rushed outside, eager to tell the crowd what had happened. And now, suddenly, everyone could understand. People from the north and from the south. People from the east and from the west. People from all around the world. For now Jesus' friends were able to speak in foreign languages – languages they had never learned – all because of God's Holy Spirit! What better way to tell the world about Jesus?

"So that's what it's all about," said a man from Spain.

"That's amazing!" said a woman from Ethiopia.

"Tell me again!" asked a man from France.

But there were others who thought Jesus' friends were just talking nonsense.

"These people are drunk!" one man shouted. "It's nothing but a load of gibberish!"

Why do you think some thought that Jesus' disciples were drunk?

And that's when Peter stood up.

Peter – who had been with Jesus from the start.

Peter – the fisherman.

Peter – who had never made a speech in his life!

"Listen, everybody!" he shouted. "We are not filled with wine. We're filled with something else – God's own Holy Spirit!

"Many years ago, a prophet said that this would happen – that God would send his Spirit to help not just special people like prophets and kings, but everyone!"

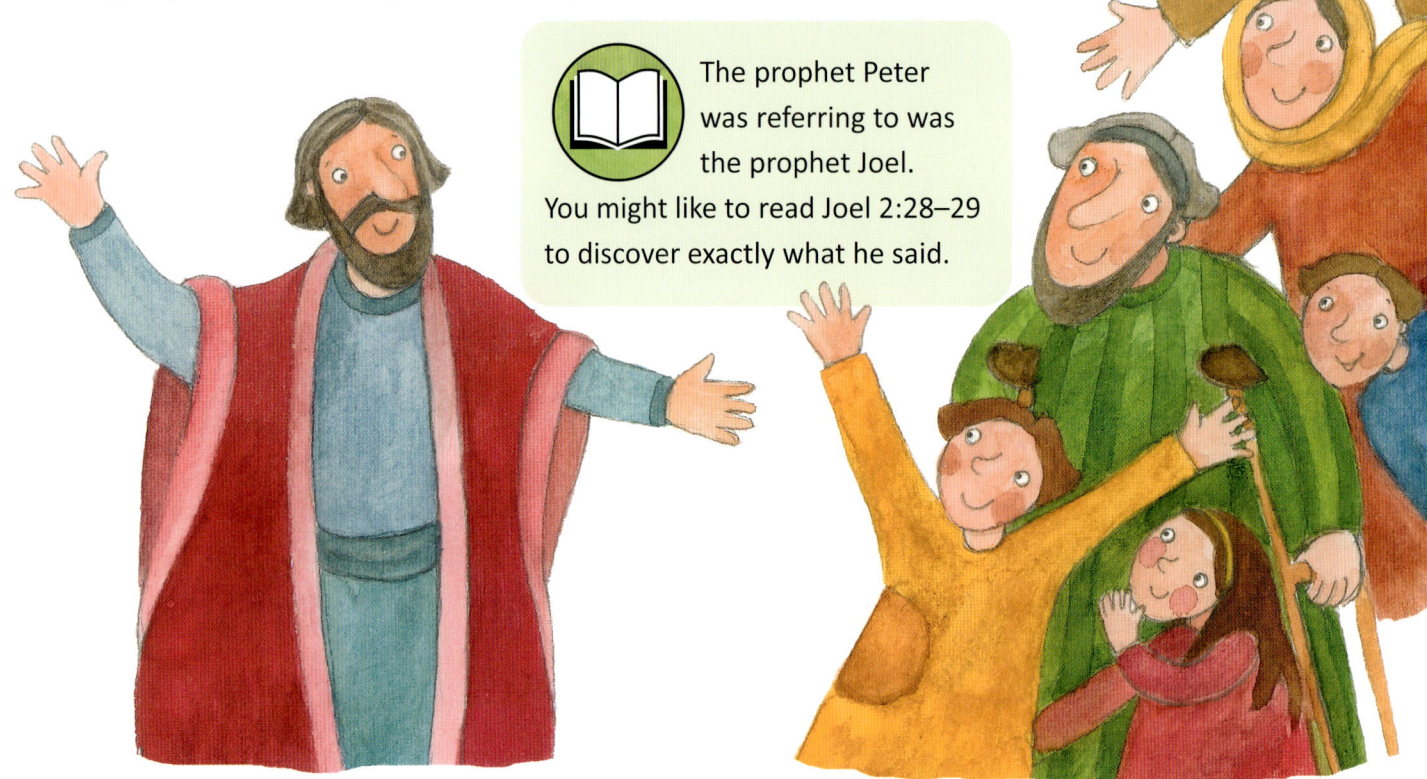

> The prophet Peter was referring to was the prophet Joel. You might like to read Joel 2:28–29 to discover exactly what he said.

"That has happened to us today. And it has happened because Jesus, who died on a cross, was brought back to life by God himself and now sits beside God in heaven! It was Jesus who sent this wonderful gift to us. Jesus, the Special One we have been waiting for all these years. Jesus, who was put to death by you."

The people were sorry for what they had done to Jesus.

"What can we do?" they cried.

"Tell God you're sorry," said Peter. "Let him wash away all the bad things you have done. And you will receive his Holy Spirit too."

So that's what the people did. Three thousand of them! They told God they were sorry. They were baptized. And they were filled with God's Holy Spirit.

Some of us were surely also in the crowd, several weeks before, that cried out for Jesus to be put to death. What was it that changed our minds and made us feel sorry for what we had done?

Why do you think I gave the people that particular set of responses when they asked what they should do? Do people still do those things today?

People from the north and from the south. People from the east and from the west. People from all over the world!

Jews from all over the world were in Jerusalem to celebrate the Feast of Pentecost, which was a kind of Harvest festival. You can read about it in Leviticus, chapter 23.

What do you think is the connection between a Harvest festival and the coming of God's Spirit?

There is a story in the Old Testament, in Genesis, chapter 11, that also involves languages. What does that story have to do with this one?

The prophet Joel said that everyone would receive God's Spirit and see visions and dream dreams. Have a look back through this book and find a story where people saw visions or dreamed dreams. Then talk about what you found.

List the relationships in this story. You will find lots of different USes. And a brand-new set of USes, in fact! How does this story illustrate the way that God turns ME into US?

You could pray that you will be attentive and obedient to the things that God's Holy Spirit wants to do in your life.

On the Road to Damascus

Hi! My name is Paul. But I used to be called Saul. I was from a place called Tarsus, in what you now call Turkey. I was trained to be a Jewish rabbi. I tried to serve God faithfully. Jesus and all his followers, at that time, were Jewish too. We just had a different idea of who the messiah was. Jesus' followers believed that he was the messiah and that God had brought him back from the dead to show that. I thought they were absolutely and completely wrong!

But in a very dramatic way, God showed me that I was the one who was wrong. It changed my life! It's a story I never tire of telling people. In fact, you can find it in the Bible in several places! The version you are about to read is from Acts, chapter 9.

When the story says that Saul didn't like Jesus, make an angry face. When it says that Jesus liked Saul, smile.

Saul did not like Jesus. Not at all.

He had never met Jesus, but he was friendly with the religious leaders who had helped put Jesus to death. And if they said Jesus was bad, that was good enough for him. Saul didn't like the people who followed Jesus either. Not one bit. When they said that Jesus was God's son, and that he had come back from the dead, it made Saul angry. He had tried to do his best for God, and believed that such things were not possible.

Make a list of the reasons why Saul did not like Jesus, or his followers.

Saul travelled up and down the country, arresting Jesus' followers, throwing them into prison, and putting them to death. The followers of Jesus were afraid, so some of them ran away – far away into other countries. But that did not stop Saul. When he heard that they had fled to the city of Damascus, he gathered his friends together and set off to arrest them. Saul did not like Jesus. Not at all.

Why do you think I thought it was all right to put people in prison and even kill them for what they believed about God? How did I get it so wrong?

But Jesus liked Saul.

Have you ever tried to make friends with someone who didn't like you?

As Saul hurried along the road to Damascus, Jesus went to meet him! He came to Saul in a vision, with a blinding flash of light so powerful that Saul fell to his knees.

"Saul," said Jesus. "Saul, why don't you like me?"

Saul was confused. He had no idea what had happened and who was talking to him. So he asked, "Who are you?" And when the answer came, Saul trembled with fear.

What do you think I thought Jesus would do to me?

"I am Jesus," said the voice in the light. "You've been hurting my friends. And when you do that, you hurt me. Here's what I want you to do: get up and go to Damascus, just as you planned. I will send a messenger to tell you what you must do."

Saul got up, but when he opened his eyes, he could not see! So his friends took him by the hand and led him into Damascus. And there he waited for three days, not eating or drinking a thing.

Try putting yourself in my place. I have been blinded by a man whose followers I have killed and imprisoned. What might have been going through my head as I waited those three days?

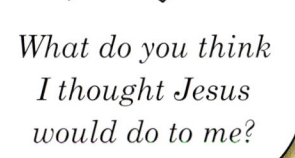

Meanwhile, Jesus spoke to one of his friends in Damascus – a man named Ananias.

"Ananias," he said, "go to Straight Street. A man named Saul is staying there. He's blind, and I want you to heal him."

"Saul?" cried Ananias. "But he's the one who's been arresting your followers and putting them to death. He doesn't like you. Not at all!"

"I know," said Jesus. "But I like Saul. And I have plans for him. I'm going to send him around the world to tell people everywhere all about me!"

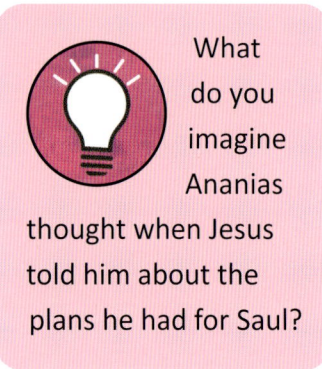

What do you imagine Ananias thought when Jesus told him about the plans he had for Saul?

So Ananias went. He laid his hands on Saul and once again, Saul could see. What is more, Saul decided there and then to follow Jesus too. He was baptized, filled with the Holy Spirit, and, some time later, to show that he was a new person he even took a new name.

"You can call me Paul, from now on," he said.

And Paul never grew tired of telling people that the man he hadn't liked, liked him anyway, and had given him another chance.

He never grew tired of talking about Jesus. Not at all.

Why do you think Paul decided to follow Jesus? Why did Jesus choose Paul to travel around the world and tell people about him?

Ananias played a really important role in Paul's story. Who has played an important part in your story by showing you something about God?

Do you know anyone whose life has been changed dramatically by Jesus, like Paul's was? Talk about it.

List the positive relationships in this story – the USes. Are there any places where US makes a difference to ME?

You could pray for someone who doesn't like you or someone you don't like. Ask God to show you a way to make things better between you.

The Earth Shakes

Hi! It's Paul here again! After I met Jesus on the Damascus Road, I told everyone I could all about him. The people who once liked me were horrified by the change. Even the followers of Jesus were suspicious. Who could blame them? But one of them, a man called Barnabas, supported me. So he and I took a trip through Asia Minor (what is now Turkey) to tell people about Jesus. In each town, we told the message first to Jewish people, people like us.

Then we told the story of Jesus to people who weren't Jewish, people we called Gentiles. It was the special job that God had planned for me all along. Later I went on another trip, with a man called Silas. That trip took us into Europe, into what is now Greece. But in the city of Philippi, we ran into a little trouble! You can read the story in Acts, chapter 16.

When you hear the word "trapped", wrap your arms around your body as if you are tied up.

The little girl was trapped – taken over by a demon and also by her human masters, who used the powers the demon gave her to make themselves a fortune.

"She'll tell your future!" they shouted to the crowds in Philippi. "And she'll tell you the meaning of your dreams as well! Just put your money on the table!"

Then Paul and Silas came to town to tell everyone about Jesus. And when she saw them, the slave girl shouted, "These men are the servants of the Most High God."

Her words were true, but Paul was worried about the poor girl, and worried as well that the crowd would think his message had something to do with the evil power inside her.

So Paul told the demon, "In the name of Jesus, come out!"

And it left the girl that very second!

That should have been the end of the story. But the girl's two masters could see that she would bring them no money. They were very angry. So they had Paul and Silas beaten and thrown into prison.

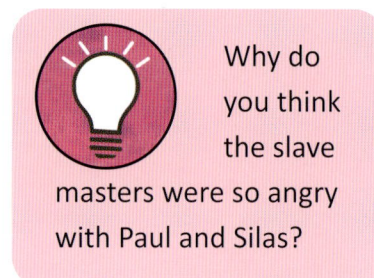

Why do you think the slave masters were so angry with Paul and Silas?

Now Paul and Silas were trapped! Their cell door was locked. Their feet were in stocks. They were stuck in a foreign jail.

They might have complained. They might have cursed. But instead they prayed and sang praises to God.

And, almost at once, God answered their prayers.

Shaking and quaking and making much noise, an earthquake broke into their song. Shaking and quaking and breaking the locks, an earthquake broke open their cell. And then, shaking and quaking and taking his sword, the jailer went to kill himself. For the law was clear – if the prisoners escaped, he would have to die in their place.

How do you think the prisoners felt when everything started shaking? And after that, when their prison doors flew open?

Now the jailer was trapped! And

How do you think we managed to keep everyone from running away?

Why do you think we prayed and sang praises to God instead of complaining?

there was no way out but death! Or so he thought.

For that's when Paul shouted: "Don't hurt yourself! We're all here."

Shaking and quaking and taking his torch, the jailer went to see. Paul was right. No one had escaped! The jailer fell to his knees.

"I've heard you sing. I've heard you pray. I've seen the saving power of your God. So tell me," he said to Paul and Silas, "what must I do to be saved?"

So Paul and Silas told him about Jesus. How he'd died on the cross and come to life again. How this had set everyone free from the power of evil and the fear of death.

The jailer believed what they told him, and he and all his family were baptized.

And now no one – not the girl, not Paul and Silas, not the jailer and his family – was trapped any more!

What different things might I have meant when I asked, "What must I do to be saved?"

Paul and Silas were punished for doing something good. Name someone, from history perhaps or even someone you know, who got into trouble because they had done something good.

Have you ever felt trapped by anything? What happened to make you feel free again? Did Jesus have anything to do with that?

List the relationships in this story. Were all of them good? Was anyone more concerned with ME than with US?

Pray for people who feel trapped by something in their lives. Ask God for the wisdom to know how to help them.

New Heaven, New Earth

> Hi! My name is John. Many of Jesus' followers were persecuted for telling people about him. Some were even killed. But I was sent to an Island called Patmos, off the coast of Greece. That is where Jesus came to me, in a vision, to show me all that God was doing and would one day do. This is what I saw, just before that vision came to an end.

This earth, the earth we live on, came to an end. It passed away. The sky did too. And the seas.

But in their place, God made another earth and sky and sea. A brand-spanking-new place for us to live.

And then, down from heaven, came a new Jerusalem too. God's Holy

City. It was beautiful, so beautiful! Beautiful as a bride, dressed to meet her husband.

I heard something next. A voice. A loud booming voice. It came from a throne. And what it said was this:

"Look! See! God is going to make his home with women and with men. He will be their God. They will be his people. And this is what he is going to do.

"He will wipe the tears from their eyes, that's what. Because everything that once made them cry – death and mourning and pain – will disappear!"

"I'm making everything new!" That's what the One on the throne says. "For I am the Alpha and the Omega. I am the beginning and I am the end. And to all who are thirsty, I freely give the water of life!"

People sometimes have the idea that we are meant to live in heaven after we die. But the vision Jesus gave John paints a different picture. A picture of a new world for us to live in. A new world made by God, where he lives with us closely. What do you think is the best thing about this new world, as John describes it? What is the most surprising thing? What is the most confusing thing?

Think back to the first few chapters of this book. Are there any places described there that this reminds you of?

Alpha is the first letter in the Greek alphabet (look, there it is again, in the very word we still use to describe our set of letters!). Omega is the last letter. It's the same as saying that God is the beginning and the end. But what does that mean? How is God the beginning and the end?

There are a great many USes brought together here – relationships put back together for ever. List them, if you can. Look through all the lists that you have written.

You could say a prayer of thanks to God for making a beautiful place where we will live for ever.